I0418867

Art in Hong Kong

Hot Topics in the Art World

Published in association with Sotheby's Institute of Art

Series Editors

Jeffrey Boloten and Juliet Hacking, Sotheby's Institute of Art, London

This series of short, thought-provoking and sometimes controversial books debates key issues of current relevance to art-world professionals working in both the private and public sectors. The texts give wider visibility to some critical areas of professional art-world practice, considering what disruptors are challenging the status quo and how the art world is likely to be transformed over the next decades as a result.

International Series Advisory Board

Georgina Adam, journalist, author and art market Editor-at-Large of *The Art Newspaper*

Alia Al-Senussi, cultural strategist, patron, academic and lecturer

Touria El Glaoui, Founding Director of 1-54 Contemporary African Art Fair (London – New-York – Marrakech)

Jos Hackforth-Jones, former CEO and Director of Sotheby's Institute of Art, London

Louise Hamlin, Director of the Art Business Conference (London – New York – Shanghai)

Llucià Homs, Director of Talking Galleries, Barcelona

Zehra Jumabhoy, academic, critic and curator

Julie Lomax, CEO at a-n, The Artists Information Company, UK

Franklin Sirmans, Director of the Pérez Art Museum, Miami

Philip Tinari, Director and CEO of the UCCA Center for Contemporary Art, Beijing

Art in Hong Kong

Portrait of a City in Flux

Enid Tsui

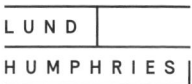

LUND
HUMPHRIES

Sotheby's INSTITUTE OF ART

First published in 2025 by Lund Humphries
in association with Sotheby's Institute of Art

Lund Humphries
Second Home Spitalfields
68–80 Hanbury Street
London E1 5JL
UK
www.lundhumphries.com

Art in Hong Kong: Portrait of a City in Flux © Enid Tsui, 2025
All rights reserved

ISBN (hardback): 978-1-84822-667-8
ISBN (eBook PDF): 978-1-84822-669-2
ISBN (eBook ePub): 978-1-84822-668-5

A Cataloguing-in-Publication record for this book is available from the
British Library

All rights reserved. No part of this publication may be reproduced, stored
in a retrieval system or transmitted in any form or by any means, electrical,
mechanical or otherwise, without first seeking the permission of the copyright
owners and publishers. Every effort has been made to seek permission to
reproduce the images in this book. Any omissions are entirely unintentional,
and details should be addressed to the publishers.

Enid Tsui has asserted her right under the Copyright, Designs and Patents Act,
1988, to be identified as the Author of this Work.

Copy edited by Michela Parkin
Designed by Crow Books
Set in Caslon Pro and Sofia Pro
Printed in Estonia

Contents

Foreword

In this pioneering new study, leading Hong Kong-based journalist Enid Tsui explodes the myth that Hong Kong's cultural scene is merely a facet of its status as a tax-free haven. Attending to the conventional view that Hong Kong was a cultural desert that embraced imported art as just one more commodity to be traded, Tsui ably demonstrates that the city did in fact foster and encourage art-making during its emergence as a global trading hub for cultural objects.

In her illuminating text based on first-hand research, Tsui examines Hong Kong's privileged place on the world stage since the late 1990s. Bringing her analysis right up to date, she explores how, in recent years, Hong Kong has pushed forward with the rapid development of the West Kowloon Cultural District and is strengthening its status as a cultural hub within the ambitious new economic zone in Southern China known as the Greater Bay Area. However, there is also concern from some sectors that the more liberal culture of the city is receding in the face of the new security laws and that its creative vigour and its position as a dynamic global art hub may be compromised.

Hong Kong's role in the global art ecosystem is a subject that is of intense interest to cultural commentators, art professionals and artists. Tsui's research and insights offer an intelligent, probing and balanced analysis of the past, present and future place of art in this city in flux.

Jeffrey Boloten and Juliet Hacking, September 2024

Acknowledgements

This book is dedicated first and foremost to the artists of Hong Kong whose brilliance is often left to burn quietly in the wilderness of art history, which nonetheless helps illuminate the paths to understanding ourselves and our city.

I wish to express my deepest gratitude to the many individuals who generously shared their insights and personal experiences for this book, thus giving shape to a place that shapeshifts often.

I am grateful to my culture desk colleagues at the *South China Morning Post*, who have provided me with a sanctuary from which I can freely and quietly consider the past and future of a contested space constantly harangued with forceful, irreconcilable prognostications.

Special thanks to David Clarke, Yeewan Koon, Johnson Chang, Suhanya Raffel, Anthony Yung, Rachel Cartland, John Batten, Tobias Berger, Jaffa Lam, Eunice Tsang, Charmaine Chan and Kevin Kwong.

Introduction

What is Hong Kong?

A newspaper editor from London once said to me: 'Hong Kong would be one of the nicest cities in the world. If only they could finish building it.' He was baffled by the constant construction in one of the most developed economies in the world. As generations of residents have discovered, the dynamism of Hong Kong's dense urban environment, as delightful as it is addictive, is all too often interrupted by the ground-shaking, bass thump of pile drivers and the penetrating buzz of electric drills.

Certain fundamentals of the city's economy, in which the property sector plays a major role, are behind the enthusiasm for construction. The constant building and redevelopment are also manifestations of the city's mercantile DNA: an organic, entrepreneurial instinct to stay on top of changes in demand and supply, and also a habit of nimble adjustments to situations brought on by forces much bigger than the city of 7.5 million people.

Those forces, invariably tied to China's vacillating relationship with the rest of the world, have been responsible for every major turning point in the city. As the most open conduit of money, goods, ideas and people between China and the rest of the world, Hong Kong has always been a strategic location for close encounters and compromises between competing economic interests and ideologies. Over the years, this open, inclusive and prosperous environment has created one of the biggest art markets in the world, some of Asia's most respected and stable cultural institutions, and a thriving, local artistic community.

Today, growing rivalry between a rising China and a US-led world order is causing global reverberations that are felt intensely in this Chinese Special Administrative Region, and raising questions about how the city's art scene is going to change, once again. This book considers those changes and how the stakes are especially high for businesses which have invested significantly in the city, and for local artists and art professionals deciding on their future. It is also aimed at anyone who wants to better understand the city's art scene beyond the usual, simplistic doom-and-gloom or all-is-well narratives.

The title of this book refers to the inherent mutability of Hong Kong, which has become particularly pronounced in the years since 2019. Recent convergence of seemingly opposing forces has seen unprecedented prominence given to the arts, while the post-2019 protest, post-Covid pandemic political reality brings unfamiliar scrutiny and restrictions. I want to show that the outcome has yet to be decided. That there is no formula for success has to do with the city's uniqueness. After all, it is a historic anomaly – a rare case of a former colony which did not become independent during the rise of nationalism and call for autonomy after the Second World War.

Here, briefly, are some important facts about Hong Kong. The coastal city was the last significant remnant of the British empire when, on 1 July 1997, it was returned to the People's Republic of China after a peaceful, 13-year-long handover process negotiated between Beijing and London.

Stability has been a key promise since 1984, when Deng Xiaoping and Margaret Thatcher signed the 'Sino-British Joint Declaration' which assured Hong Kong that, after around 150 years of British colonial rule, it would continue to be a free trading port and retain the many freedoms of an open society as China itself was pursuing a new path of economic development which chose pragmatism over uncompromising ideology.[1] The agreement promised '50 years of no change' after the 1997 handover and that the new 'Special Administrative Region' would be governed by Communist China under a 'one country, two systems' model that would allow it a high degree of autonomy while enjoying incomparable access to China's vast market.

Hong Kong's mini constitution, called the Basic Law, enshrines the following features: Hong Kong remains the only common-law jurisdiction in China; it has its own customs territory with no customs duties imposed on imported goods; the absence of value-added or sales tax; the absence of wealth, death or capital-gains duties; its own currency, the Hong Kong dollar, which is freely convertible and has been pegged to the US dollar since 1983; freedom of speech, of the press and publication, of assembly and demonstration and other civic rights; and having both Chinese and English as official languages.

But the city has never stood still. For English readers, John Carroll's *A Concise History of Hong Kong* is required reading for anyone interested in how the city, like places abutting tectonic fault lines, is particularly exposed to the tremors caused when China and the United States rub each other up the wrong way. Just as settlers in geologically unstable areas are rewarded by the fertility of the volcanic soil under their feet, Hong Kong, too, has had reasons to be grateful to its being in a geopolitical borderland. In a chapter titled 'A New Hong Kong', Carroll details a succession of events in the 1950s and 1960s which heralded the city's transition in the second half of the 20th century from a post-Second World War backwater to a thriving economy, fuelled by an influx of labour and capital from mainland China after the 1949 Communist revolution.

That era of the Cold War and the Cultural Revolution turned the then British colony into a proxy battleground for clashing ideologies and interests, with simmering tension exploding during the widely-known riots of 1966–7. Less well known were the delicate, practical manoeuvres and compromises which led to enduring economic benefits – a historical feat which Hong Kong hopes to repeat in the 21st century amid escalating geopolitical tension.[2] Decades of strong growth turned Hong Kong into one of the 'Four Dragons of Asia' – high-income post-industrialisation economies including Singapore, Taiwan and South Korea – in the last decades of the 20th century.

Political and economic stability bred a vibrant art scene and a major market for Chinese works of art and ink paintings. International interest soared in the 2010s, due to the rise of the modern and contemporary art market that accompanied the first Art Basel Hong Kong. Hong Kong's art ecosystem has continued to mature in the years since, with more non-profit institutions coming on stream to educate, research and archive from an inclusive regional perspective that reflects Hong Kong's identity and culture.

Following what I describe in Chapter 2 as the 'Hong Kong Decade', 2019 brought dramatic rupture. A proposed extradition agreement with mainland China triggered the largest anti-government protests in the city's history, seen by Beijing as an attempt to undermine its authority. A new national security law was quickly introduced by the central government in 2020 that criminalises secession, subversion, terrorism and collusion with foreign forces in order to effectuate a more firm-handed and nationalistic rule. This coincided with three years of COVID-19 pandemic isolation as Hong Kong sealed the city borders to try to achieve 'zero Covid'. Today, culture is at the forefront of the Special Administrative Region's post-pandemic integration with the rest of China. This integration is mainly achieved through Hong Kong's incorporation into a new Greater Bay Area (GBA) that China has drawn up to try to rival the economic power and level of innovation in the San Francisco Bay Area.[3]

Subsequent to the initial IT-led economic blueprint for the GBA, published by Beijing in 2019, the new region that includes Hong Kong, Macau – the former Portuguese-owned gambling hub – and nine mainland cities has also been given a cultural mandate: to foster a shared identity and cultural heritage between Hong Kong and its Chinese neighbours, while also showing the world the most outward-facing aspect of Chinese culture given the region's long engagement with the West.[4] Meanwhile, China's 14th five-year plan in 2020 made Hong Kong an 'East-meets-West Centre for International Cultural Exchange' and ordered the city to 'tell good stories of China' through the arts.[5] Domestically, the Hong Kong administration is also trying to boost patriotism by promoting Chinese culture after the 2019 anti-government protests.[6]

The city's vibrant art scene is also part of the government's post-pandemic push to lure back tourists, investors and international talents. This has seen the establishment of a new government bureau in charge of culture and tourism and a new 'Mega Arts and Cultural Events Fund'. The city's recent political transformation and growing integration with the GBA are prompting much soul-searching in a city that has always defined itself by how different it is from China, and with it, questions about its future as an international arts centre.

Artists and art professionals need to be aware of what the new political reality means for them (which I shall examine in Chapter 5). Hong Kong's unassailability as the region's top art market was dented by its pandemic isolation, but it is far too early to dismiss Hong Kong's art scene as a has-been. As this book will illustrate, there remains a well-informed, open-minded and diverse community behind a potent art sector that provides valuable perspectives on the epochal shifts that are shaping the 21st century. The art-market sector is bullish, with new models of business bolstering and upgrading what the city has to offer, while the number of billionaires and private museums continues to grow within the GBA. Meanwhile, a new, exciting crop of local galleries and art spaces has appeared, backed by energetic and passionate individuals who are highly collaborative and are now supported by world-class new institutions such as M+ (which is the focus of Chapter 4).

The constant pounding of pile drivers may be a pain but better the noise of redevelopment, which at least gives hope for renewal, than the silence of statis.

1

Art in Hong Kong

The Immigrant Artist

Jaffa Lam's story of her childhood as a new immigrant in Hong Kong and how she came to be represented by a major international gallery is a tale with dramatic turning points underpinned by an unwavering self-belief. It is also a story that helps elucidate recurring themes in this book: Hong Kong's perforated relationship with China, the dynamics behind its own art history, the impact of the international art market and, most of all, that there is no such thing as a straightforward, linear Hong Kong narrative.

Lam was born in 1973 in Fujian province, southern China, while Mao Zedong's Great Proletarian Cultural Revolution was still raging. Lam was given the Chinese first name Laam, which means mountain mist, but she never had the luxury of living with her head in the clouds. Lam's mother took her and her sister to Hong Kong in 1985, initially to reunite with their father who had moved earlier to the British colony. But the years of separation had taken their toll on the marriage, so Lam, her elder sister and her mother ended up living on their own again and were soon plunged into abject poverty.

Hong Kong in 1985 was just coming to terms with the fact that Britain was planning to hand it over to Communist China in 1997 after ruling it since 1842. But the economy was remarkably resilient, underpinned by Beijing's promise that Hong Kong could keep its capitalist ways, retain its civic freedoms and enjoy a high degree of autonomy. As immigrants from China, the family had to adapt to a completely different way of life, a different way of writing Chinese (traditional rather than simplified characters), a different way of speaking (Cantonese, rather than Mandarin) and, in an expensive city where they could only afford to rent a tiny rooftop shack, a different class system altogether.

For all the dazzling economic achievements under the British colonial government, Hong Kong's free-market status is responsible for its extreme wealth disparity – it is one of the most unequal places in the world.[1] 'I had the grades to move to a better school in Hong Kong but my mother was worried that I would be looked down on by wealthier classmates whose families would all have private cars and be able to go abroad for holidays', Lam recalls.[2] Money was so tight that Lam had to work part-time as a young teenager in garment factories.

Art was not so much an escape as a means to help out the household budget. 'I had taken art lessons in China so I was quite a good art student compared with my local classmates. I kept winning school prizes – textbook vouchers, usually, which were really helpful. That's how I came to think of art as a means of making a living', she confesses. Her exemplary skills in drawing and calligraphy won her admission to Hong Kong's only fine art tertiary programme then, at the Chinese University of Hong Kong (CUHK). She intended to focus on Chinese calligraphy under the school's many eminent ink masters. 'I thought of myself as an inheritor of China's literati tradition. I had no idea about Western art history or contemporary art', she recalls. She discovered that her attitude and worldview were out of tune with her locally educated classmates, who did not identify as closely with traditional Chinese culture. Lam says she thought she had more in common with a proud lineage of Chinese artists and intellectuals who moved to the city during periods of great turmoil on the mainland.

Hong Kong was a safe haven for eminent sinologists and philosophers such as Ch'ien Mu and Jao Tsung-I, who moved to the then British colony when the Communists took control of China in 1949. Later, the influx of talent fleeing the Cultural Revolution resulted in a golden age of the arts. Among those who decamped to the city were painters such as Lui Shou-kwan and his cohort, who pioneered the 'New Ink Painting Movement' in the 1960s and 1970s in Hong Kong.[3] They injected fresh vigour into a traditional Chinese art genre by amalgamating elements of Western abstract art, mirroring the cross-cultural fertilisation between Zen Buddhism and Abstract Expressionists working in America in the same period.

The impact of the émigré artists, writers and intellectuals was so great that Hong Kong developed an inferiority complex about the value of its own culture that continues to torment the city from time to time. The contemporary novelist John Chan Koon-chung has traced the earliest record of the phrase 'a cultural desert' to a 1920s article by Lu Xun. By writing 'Hong Kong is not a cultural desert', one of the greatest writers of the 20th century condemned the city to being called one for generations to come, Chan claims.[4] Generations of government officials have since used the term to emphasise the transformative nature of new cultural projects. For example, in 2023, Executive Councillor Jeffrey Lam Kin-fung said in an interview that the West Kowloon Cultural District would help convince mainland Chinese visitors that Hong Kong was not a cultural desert.[5]

One enduring misconception is that Hong Kong had no art before the 1960s, in spite of plenty of evidence showing otherwise. The 19th-century Chinese artist Lamqua, inspired by the master of trade art George Chinnery and who exhibited at the Royal Academy in London twice, set up a thriving commercial studio in Hong Kong just after the British arrived in 1842.[6] An early wave of immigrant artists arrived in the 1930s, including overseas Chinese trained in Western art schools such as Li Tiefu and Li Bing.

But the 1960s did draw many artists from far and wide, as Hong Kong's economy began to take off. Painters such as Douglas Bland, Rosamond Brown and Brian Tilbrook (who is still active as an artist and lives in Hong Kong) fused elements from their new and old lives while keeping to Western materials and techniques. Another group of artists, made up of largely ethnic Chinese artists who grew up in Hong Kong and learned both Chinese and Western techniques, gradually developed their own independent visual languages. This group, comprising artists such as Luis Chan, Hon Chi-fun, Irene Chou and Cheung Yee, was at the heart of a 'boisterous art decade' that British art critic Nigel Cameron discovered when he moved to Hong Kong in the 1960s.[7] Regardless of their place of birth, these artists were exhibiting as 'Hong Kong artists' internationally by the 1960s.[8]

Before the Handover

Being a Hong Kong artist acquired further meaning when Lam was in art school at CUHK in the 1990s. Her peers were discussing Postmodernism and postcolonial critique ahead of the 1997 handover to China. Local artists were abandoning what they perceived to be the cultural essentialism of the Chinese ink tradition as well as the aesthetic autonomy of Western Modernism, and preferring to make conceptual art and site-specific installations that reflected a desire to engage with the place they were in.

In the 1990s, mainland Chinese artists were witnessing changes brought on by the country's euphoric embrace of international trade and privatisation, but artists in Hong Kong did not have the luxury of engaging in that brief, worldwide delusion that Cold War-era ideological conflicts were a thing of the past.[9] Faced with imminent absorption into a rising global power, local artists were urgently articulating a distinctive identity and directly confronting sources of tension in the British colony: the unequal relationship between metropole and periphery, the injustice of capitalism, the tug-of-war between East and West.

A 1990 exhibition called *In Search of Art* at the Hong Kong Arts Centre invited residents to share their personal art collections. Co-organisers David Clarke, an artist and art historian at the University of Hong Kong, and artist-curator Oscar Ho Hing-kay, HKAC's then exhibition director, originally intended the exercise to be a counter-hegemonic initiative to challenge the distinction between high and low art.[10] It developed into a series of exhibitions which sought to 'nurture and identify a Hong Kong cultural identity', as Ho wrote.[11] One of the exhibitions opened on the night before the handover, on 30 June 1997. Called *Hong Kong Incarnated – Museum 97: History, Community, Individual*, it featured a large number of artworks made to respond to the handover, including a temple with a door that said: 'You're on Your Own – Good Luck!' – reflecting the not uncommon feeling at the time that Hong Kong was being abandoned by Britain and not given a say in its future.

But the most enduring image was perhaps a new and powerful symbol of the city – the aptly amphibian and indigenous 'Lo Ting'. Eccentric, unique and biologically ambivalent, these half-human, half-fish creatures were presented as sculptures and in paintings and texts. Being 'in-between', Lo Tings were able to survive and roam between two different worlds, the embodiment of a typical Hong Konger, Ho explained.[12] These strange creatures with a fish's head have become an enduring avatar which keeps reappearing in plays, films and other exhibitions, a symbol of the desire for self-definition beyond the narratives controlled by official Chinese and British histories. That desire is also the result of an absence that distinguished Hong Kong from other postcolonial societies: the absence of an ethnic or national narrative separate from that of its new master, China, or an independent symbol of high culture that existed before the British came. Hong Kong artists make up their own myths.[13]

The uncertainty and helplessness at the time of the handover is palpable in a number of works by the city's first generation of feminist experimental artists such as Ellen Pau and May Fung, two of the co-founders of the non-profit video art collective Videotage in 1986, and Linda Lai, who taught for many years at the City University of Hong Kong and founded the independent art space Floating Projects. Fung's *She Said Why Me* (1989), now in the M+ museum collection, was made immediately after the Tiananmen Square crackdown in Beijing on 4 June, an event which prompted a massive crisis of confidence and an exodus that saw many Hong Kong families resettle in countries such as Canada and Australia. It is a seven-and-a-half-minute video showing a blindfolded woman as she feels her way through the busy streets and historic landmarks. This video is interspersed with historic footage of women in public spaces, prompting a rethinking of female history in a patriarchal, colonial society.

Poignantly, Fung made a new work of the same title in 2016, showing herself and another woman seemingly out of place, and out of sync, with their own city – a reflection of the growing sense of alienation amid the rapid political transformation in the Chinese Special Administrative Region.

The Hong Kong condition, of being in between two major national powers and occupying what postcolonial cultural theorist Homi Bhabha terms a 'third space', is something which has fascinated scholars. One of the most often quoted concepts about the city's interstitial qualities – and how that puts Hong Kong culture in constant danger of being overlooked – is Ackbar Abbas's idea of 'déjà disparu' (already disappeared). He explains in his 1994 paper 'The New Hong Kong Cinema and the "Déjà Disparu"' that: 'The threat will be that Hong Kong as a subject will be presented and represented in terms of some of the old *binarisms* whose function it is to restabilize differences and domesticate change, for example, binarisms like East and West, or tradition and modernity.'[14]

Indeed, it has been observed that Hong Kong art has rarely been included in exhibitions of Chinese contemporary art before or after the handover.[15] It is not just because China is a big country. Writing in 1999, Oscar Ho warned that art that highlighted a distinct Hong Kong culture was problematic to the city's rulers: 'During the transitional period, talking about a distinctive Hong Kong culture was in fact

politically dangerous. For cultural autonomy implied political autonomy, and there was nothing more irritating to Beijing than talking
about independence.'[16]

Art and Society

Meanwhile, art education in the 1990s was heavily influenced by
returnees who had studied and lived in the West. Taught by artists such
as Choi Yan-chi (born 1949), Kurt Chan (born 1959) and Ho Siu-kee
(born 1964), Hong Kong's majority ethnic Chinese artists increasingly
exhibited an 'interiorisation' of a hybrid culture that often made the
boundary between East and West so blurred as to be invisible, as art
historian Frank Vigneron writes.[17]

It is important to note that there was not a complete rejection of
traditional Chinese art in the 1990s (or now). New Ink Art pioneers
Lui Shou-kwan and Liu Kuo-sung taught for years in local universities
and their influences can still be seen.[18] In fact, historians have pointed
out that the British colonial government encouraged the study of traditional Chinese culture at school, in a way that promoted a Chinese
identity in the abstract, one where the nationalism and patriotism in
the People's Republic of China and Taiwan were redacted.[19]

Neither is the art community wholly Chinese. Given Hong Kong's
lack of space, it is not really a city that artists elsewhere would look to
if they want to set up a studio. But besides British artists who followed
the empire to Hong Kong earlier, the commercial sector and the education sector, especially at a tertiary level, continue to create opportunities
for artists who don't mind juggling their studio work with a day job.

Lam had to find her own way. At first, she was only interested in
becoming a better Chinese calligrapher. Her fellow undergraduates
were not impressed. 'I was laughed at. Fellow students thought I was
dumb to just want to do calligraphy', she says. In her third year (1995),
Lam stumbled across a sculpture course with the late Cheung Yee, one
of Hong Kong's early Modernist artists, who appreciated Lam's interest
in Chinese antiquity. He would take Lam along to Sun Chau Book &

Antique Co. to discuss connoisseurship, while also obliquely pointing out to her that art was more than technique.

Cheung's mentorship rubbed off. Lam was selected for the 1996 Contemporary Hong Kong Art Biennial Exhibition at the Hong Kong Museum of Art with a work which saw her breaking free from past influences.[20] *Clerical Script in 'Black Tiger' Style* was still calligraphic, but she added sketches to the characters to depict Tsing Ma Bridge, a major infrastructure project which signalled, then, a new era for Hong Kong before its 1 July 1997 handover to China. 'I was fed up with just copying other people's calligraphy. It really felt like my own creation. There was no way I was going back to pure calligraphy after that', Lam says.

After she finished her MFA Lam could only find work teaching art part-time in a kindergarten that barely covered the monthly university fees repayment. Like many struggling artists in Hong Kong, she shared a small studio with several other artists in a factory building and worked towards her dream of making large-scale sculptures that would really make an impact. Another major turning point was in 2003, when the Sars pandemic hit Hong Kong hard. 'Teaching work had stopped. I had hurt my leg but because of the pandemic I couldn't go to the hospital. I just sat in the studio bleeding. I felt so low. So I began working on a series of sculptures, which ended up being called *To Someone Who Wants to Cry*, *To Someone Who Wants to Run*, *To Someone Who Wants to Hide* and *To Someone Who Wants to Fly*. From then on, I only make art that is related to society', she says.

The four pieces were shown in Lam's first solo exhibition, *Murmur*, at the Shatin Town Hall in 2003. They were early examples of a quiet monumentality that has come to be a signature of her public art, and of her alchemistic ability to transform mundane, abandoned material into elegant and highly finished forms. The smallest was *To Someone Who Wants to Cry*, an identical pair of three metre-long, narrow, blond wood vessels tapered at both ends like a canoe. The sunken centres, coloured turquoise, were filled with water – the tears referenced in the work's title. The largest was *To Someone Who Wants to Hide*, an eight-metre-long zoomorphic, flattened tunnel which would be the perfect hiding place for someone who just wanted the ground to swallow them up.

A Local Identity

What Lam's practice evolved into was, in a way, Hong Kong art. I use the term with reservation, as there obviously is no one type of Hong Kong art. But compared with her early desire to carry on a timeless ideal of Chinese cultural traditions, her Tsing Ma Bridge and Sars pandemic projects reflect two common strategies used by contemporary practitioners: the moving away from any paradigmatic or overt symbols of a national discourse; and a foregrounding, if not elevation, of the plebeian, the banal and the individualistic Hong Kong experience that rings truer than top-down, clichéd descriptions of the city being a harmonious East-meets-West crossroads and a successful international financial centre.[21] One can look at how the painter Yeung Tong-lung (born 1956) lovingly treats mundane, overlooked aspects of Hong Kong street life; how sculptor Leelee Chan (born 1994) scavenges for discarded industrial materials around the city, such as plastic pellets, and transforms them into elaborate, unexpected assemblages that reflect an anti-consumerist ethos; or how Trevor Yeung (born 1988) turned the modest tropical fish shops in Mongkok into a rich critique of anthropocentrism and poetic symbol of Hong Kong society for his solo presentation at the 2024 Venice Biennale.

As for straying from a national discourse, one interesting example is Chui Pui-chee (born 1980). Although he expresses himself through traditional Chinese forms of painting and calligraphy, he upsets cultural hierarchy by rejecting, say, the scholarly and grandiloquent expressions that calligraphers traditionally convey. In a long-running series, he covers scrolls in elegantly written lyrics of local Cantonese pop songs. And then there are artists who, like Angela Su, keep parts of their practices inscrutable in terms of any national, ethnic and even generational characteristics. That obscuration of identifiable cultural markers can itself be seen as a very Hong Kong strategy.[22]

Anthony Yung, a senior researcher at the Asia Art Archive, observes that Hong Kong art's refusal to be pinned down extends to how Hong Kong art history is written versus mainland Chinese art history, which is more easily seen to correlate with the country's dramatic transformations:

Periodising is a traditional approach to writing art history. But periodisation cannot be applied to Hong Kong because there is no dominant style in each era. Hong Kong has big landmarks in its history, just like China. But local artists tend not to respond so directly. It is not to do with self-censorship. It is to do with artists making art for themselves, rather than to communicate with others[23]

This tendency for understatement, which in some ways explains the city's mislabelling as a 'cultural desert', is also underlined by what art historian Winnie Wong describes as the 'smallness in form, size, scale, and expression' of Hong Kong art. This is partly due to the city's lack of space and also may be a sign of a broader refusal of reductive geopolitics which an open, yet permanently dependent territory is constantly buffeted by.[24]

Not all Hong Kong art is a private, secretive language. For example, we saw an outpouring of protest art emerging during major social upheavals such as the protests in 2014 and 2019, as will be discussed later in the book.[25] And there is also a large group of artists whose practices include aspects of social engagement and activism related to the worsening economic and social inequality in a city which was built by the British colonial administration on the principle of minimal government intervention in the free market.[26]

From 2003, Lam became one such artist along with many others such as Leung Mee-ping (born 1961) and Luke Ching Chin-wai (born 1972). She frequently collaborates with female factory workers – a relationship developed since she was young – and one particularly memorable result was *Trolley Party* (2023), an unmissable art installation at Art Basel

Hong Kong that featured a giant canopy made with recycled umbrella fabric. Sitting beneath it in the first edition of the art fair since the COVID-19 pandemic, one felt it was a particularly apt setting for a work that highlights the value of a culture of care. Unfortunately, it did not sell.

A Niche Market

In 2018 the female artist and scholar Anthony Leung Po-shan published a book in Chinese called *I Love Art Basel*.[27] The title was an ironic response to the launch of Art Basel Hong Kong in 2012 and the subsequent arrival of multinational galleries eager to sell Western art to wealthy Asian collectors. The art 'boom' merely saw the low-tax trading hub used for transactions of commoditised international art favoured by investors, she pointed out. The city and its own culture were merely a sideshow.

As art researcher Yung also points out, it remains incredibly hard to be an artist in Hong Kong because of the high cost of living, the lack of space and the lack of an international collector base. 'That is why the artist Kwan Sheung-chi filled exercise books with the phrase "I am Artist" in English and Chinese for his 2003–4 series. It was like a mantra he had to keep repeating to himself because it is so hard to be one', he says.[28] The art historian David Clarke has highlighted another aspect of Hong Kong art that makes a lot of local art that much harder to sell: most artists don't make paintings or sculptures. Clarke explains that there is a strong tradition of installation, photography and video art that emerged from the 1990s because of a strong desire to project site and temporal specificity.[29] Two exemplary works of art from that time are Ho Siu-kee's *Walking on Two Balls* (1995), in which the artist is seen to do, with great difficulty, what the title describes, and Ellen Pau's *Diversion* (1990), a video made in the wake of the 1989 Tiananmen Square crackdown, with scenes of a large group of people jumping into the sea and a Cantonese title meaning 'caught between a rock and a hard place'.

Lam, on the other hand, was making sculptures, but not the kind that had much of a market: large, often collaborative projects that were primarily commissioned for non-selling exhibitions or as public art. Her storage space became filled up with unsold or uncollected pieces that were sent back after exhibitions. In 2022 she felt she had had enough. In an interview with journalist Oliver Giles, she recounted how she planned to spend her 50th birthday burning all her works:

> Jaffa Lam spent last year planning a major event for her upcoming 50th birthday: she was going to gather all the unsold art cluttering her studio, everything that she had made over her 22 years of working as an artist, and burn it. 'I saw no hope', she says. 'Occasionally someone would invite me to take part in a group show, but afterwards the work would always be sent back to me. No one wanted to buy it. I was so frustrated. I thought, 'This is enough. I need to take a break. I don't want to be an artist.'[30]

In a wonderful turnaround, she received a much-needed morale boost just before she lit the match. Like the turning point for her practice in 2003, this too was virus-induced. International galleries which did not sell Hong Kong art before began to look locally during the pandemic when the city's borders were shut. In 2021 Lam was one of the artists in a group show guest curated by Chris Wan at Axel Vervoordt's outpost in Wong Chuk Hang, a large space inside one of the district's many factory buildings that are homes to art galleries.

She expected the exhibition to be a one-off and that little would come of it. But the Belgian gallery has a history of representing artists who use unusual materials and methods, such as South Korean conceptual artist Kimsooja. Just before Lam turned 50, the Hong Kong gallery director Mariko Kawashima called Lam and said they would sign her and give her a solo show. Since then, exhibition invitations have been coming thick and fast. She says:

I am determined not to waste this opportunity. During Hong Kong's supposed golden age I felt I was going nowhere. Now, I feel there is still a lot that can be done by artists, such as teaching others to think like us, to see the world not as black and white. And to tell children growing up in poor families, art is for you, too. Look at me. I haven't starved to death yet!

Lam's career is like Hong Kong. It is resilient, and full of surprises.

2

'Cultural Desert' No More

As the previous chapter indicates, Hong Kong was never devoid of culture, but until the 1970s it lacked museums, art schools, commercial galleries and other vital elements of a rich and diverse cultural ecosystem. This lack of investment in the first 130 years of Britain's 155-year rule had to do with the country's practical attitude towards a colony, according to local theatre veteran and former university professor Vicki Ooi:

> The notion that the best cultural policy is no cultural policy is a direct offshoot of the general policy of *laissez-faire* established by the British colonial government since it colonised Hong Kong in 1842. Effectively it allowed the market forces to decide what to offer the people and since Hong Kong had been gained as a way into the lucrative China trade, arts and culture were placed low in priority.[1]

The new generation of world-class art institutions which arrived after 2018, such as M+ and Tai Kwun, certainly marked a new level of maturity for Hong Kong's art ecosystem and an unprecedented investment in cultural facilities, as we will see in later chapters. But they were not bolts from the blue.

The MacLehose Years

The 1970s marked a major turning point in Britain's approach to ruling Hong Kong. In 1966 and 1967 anger over dire living and working conditions as well as widespread corruption erupted into the open. The chaos and violence of the Cultural Revolution across the border was also threatening to spill over to the colony.[2] The Murray MacLehose administration (1971–82) introduced major social reform as Britain began to take seriously the need to build social cohesion and a local sense of belonging in the colony. This was despite the fact that, by 1969, the British government had decided internally that the transfer of Hong Kong to China was unavoidable.[3]

As mentioned in the Introduction, the Hong Kong economy took off after the Second World War and later made the transition from manufacturing to services, becoming an international financial centre greatly aided by China's economic opening up in 1978. The new wealth led to more funding for the arts, much of which was administered by the Urban Council, an autonomous body wholly made up of members of the public from 1973 until its dissolution in 1999.[4]

In 1975 the City Hall Museum and Art Gallery, founded in 1962, was split into the Hong Kong Museum of History and the Hong Kong Museum of Art. The plan was to move both from Central to the other side of Victoria Harbour as part of the new Tsim Sha Tsui cultural complex, located in the southern tip of the Kowloon Peninsula. That project was much delayed by budget overruns and a weak economy.[5] So it was not until 1991 that the Hong Kong Museum of Art finally moved into its current venue on the waterfront.

The 'LCSD Museums'

The Hong Kong Museum of Art, and its predecessor at the City Hall, was the main public museum dedicated to the visual arts for nearly sixty years. Its collection of 18,800 art pieces and artefacts highlights the museum's local focus, with many of the pieces donated by local artists and collectors and belonging to four main categories: Modern and Contemporary Hong Kong Art, Chinese Antiquities, Chinese Painting and Calligraphy, and China Trade Art.[6] It belongs to the dozens of publicly funded museums run by bureaucrats at the Leisure and Cultural Services Department (LCSD), which in 2000 took over the role from the Urban Council and another municipal body called the Regional Council. In 2000, too, the Hong Kong Heritage Museum opened with a significant visual-arts component, including a free permanent gallery dedicated to the influential Lingnan School artist Chao Shao-an (1905–98).

These public museums with extremely low (or no) admission fees have played an invaluable role in art education. The Hong Kong Museum of Art regularly hosts and adapts major touring exhibitions for a local audience, and from 1975 to 2013 it held the Hong Kong Contemporary Art Biennial (renamed the Hong Kong Contemporary Art Awards in its final year). In 2019 the museum reopened with a new annex and now offers upgraded facilities and far more pleasant public spaces, including a stunning view of the harbour. It has also received major donations of Chinese ink art and calligraphy since then.

The Independent Non-profits

Well before the arrival of M+ (see Chapter 4), these municipal museums were supplemented by a long line of independent non-profit venues that provided more room for experimentation and specialisation.

I have already mentioned the Hong Kong Arts Centre, a multi-purpose building founded in 1977 as a non-profit organisation 'of the people, for the people and by the people'.[7] Other bastions of the art scene which appeared before 2019 include artist-run spaces such as Videotage (founded in 1986 by May Fung, Ellen Pau, Wong Chi-fai and Comyn Mo), one of Asia's oldest non-profit new-media art groups. Veteran experimental artists, educators and curators Choi Yan-chi and Linda Lai Chiu-han were among the founders of 1a space (in 1998) and Floating Project (in 2010) respectively. Para Site was originally established in 1996 by seven artists, including Leung Chi-wo, Phoebe Man Ching-ying, Sara Wong Chi-hang and Leung Mee-ping, amid intense interest in local cultural identity ahead of the handover. Over the years, it has evolved under different directors. For example, under Cosmin Costinas (2011–22), it regularly hosted biennale-style mega exhibitions in the absence of an official Hong Kong biennale, bringing an enormous number of artists to Hong Kong for its installations and openings.

The Asia Art Archive (founded by Claire Hsu and Johnson Chang in 2000) documents the histories of art in the region and runs public programmes and a well-stocked library free for public use – indeed, this book was partly written inside its 'Hong Kong room' lined with valuable resources. WMA (founded in 2012 by the WYNG Foundation) runs an exhibition space, programmes and awards aimed at generating discussions of social issues through lens-based images. And the Asia Society, a US non-profit organisation, set up a Hong Kong centre in 2012 after beautifully restoring a historic explosives magazine perched above the central business district, regularly hosting art exhibitions with a focus on modern Chinese diasporic artists.

The Centre for Heritage, Arts and Textile (Chat) was opened in 2018. This privately funded endeavour is located within a large former factory refashioned into a cultural and lifestyle centre, and has continued to delight with a rich programme focused on local and international textile art and the genre's relationship with wider society. That same year, Tai Kwun opened in a cluster of heritage buildings that were once used as a prison, police station and a magistrates' court. Tai Kwun Contemporary, a Kunsthalle housed in the vibrant art and heritage compound, has quickly built a reputation for introducing more conceptual works, as well as live art, to a wider audience. Funding comes courtesy of the Hong Kong Jockey Club, the racing, lottery and football betting monopoly that is also the city's biggest charitable trust. The Jockey Club also paid for the Hong Kong Palace Museum, and continually supports many major exhibitions and cultural events. There are also numerous small-scale, artist-run spaces such as Hidden Space, literally hidden inside a factory building since 2017.

Where Artists Work

Given sky-high rents in Hong Kong, many artists simply work from home. But studio clusters or artist 'villages' began to appear just after the handover, as rent in the densely populated territory plunged during the Asian Financial Crisis.[8] The first to be recorded was the Oil Street artist village.[9] In 1998 artists were drawn by cheap rents to open studios in a high-ceilinged, spacious former public supplies warehouse, not far from Para Site's present-day location in North Point. This vibrant hub of creativity, which grew organically by word of mouth, lasted for three years before the artists and other tenants were evicted, despite the outcry, to make way for redevelopment.[10] Some of the Oil Street artists and collectives took up the government's offer of moving into a historic, long-vacated slaughterhouse for cattle in 2001. Those who have remained to this day include Kwok Mang-ho, a.k.a. Frog King, the performance artist who represented Hong Kong in the 2011 Venice Biennale, and the aforementioned Videotage and 1a space.

After Oil Street, artists continued to look for affordable workspace in Hong Kong's many industrial buildings increasingly vacated by the city's shrinking manufacturing sector. As artist Lam Tung-pang recalls, he and fellow classmates from the art school of the Chinese University of Hong Kong set up the first art studio in Fo Tan, a light industrial area near the university, in 2001. The name of the area, meaning fire and coal, was fitting given that the move was prompted by a fire which broke out on campus and deprived the young artists of studio space.[11] Soon other CUHK graduates followed and the annual 'Fotanian' weekends became popular with members of the public keen to see how artists work. At its peak, 260 artists opened their studios for visits over four days in 2011.

As the number of art schools and graduates grew, studio clusters began to appear in other factory areas such as Kwai Chung. One oasis of affordability in what can loosely be considered downtown Hong Kong is the *sui generis* incubator and community hub called Foo Tak Building. The 1960s high-rise, with an old-fashioned pawn shop on the ground floor (a handy source of emergency cash for any impoverished artist!), has been a haven for artists since the early 2000s. The owner asked artist May Fung (a generous mentor to young artists) to help turn the residential units into studios and rent them out at below-market prices to deserving artists. This 'vertical artist village' also houses one of the city's best art bookshops.

In 2023 the Hong Kong Arts Development Council unveiled brand new studios inside its new headquarters in Wong Chuk Hang, an industrial neighbourhood in the south side of Hong Kong Island which has the largest number of commercial galleries outside of the Central business district.

The Auctions Arrive

The Hong Kong Palace Museum, located next to M+ in the West Kowloon Cultural District, devoted one of its opening exhibitions in 2022 to the little-known history of collecting in the city. The first section introduced the earliest collectors of 'China trade art' – 18th and 19th-century Western-style watercolours, oil paintings and prints of the landscape and daily life in modern-day Guangzhou, Hong Kong and Macau. Among these collectors were early colonial Hong Kong society grandees such as Sir Paul Chater and Sir Robert Ho Tung.[12]

The bulk of collectors in the 20th century were immigrants from mainland China who brought over family heirlooms or had inherited them in Hong Kong. One of the most prominent arrivals after the 1949 Communist victory was Hu Jen-mou, previously a member of the Beijing Palace Museum's Ceramic Committee. In 1960 he co-founded the Min Chiu Society in his new home, a private gentlemen's club which to this day only accepts top Chinese art collectors into its ranks (the first and only female member was accepted as honorary member as recently as 2021).

There were also dealers who continued their family businesses that were founded in Shanghai, or Cantonese-speaking Guangzhou just across the border, mostly setting up shop along Hollywood Road and Lascar Row (popularly known as Cat Street) in Sheung Wan.

Collectors and dealers had an easier time seeking each other out after the development of the auctions market in Hong Kong from the 1970s. Julian Thompson, future Chairman of Sotheby's and head of their Chinese department at the time, decided to conduct sales in Asia after noticing the growing number of Asians in the London auctions.

Japan was still in the middle of its post-war 'economic miracle' then. Christie's had its first Asia sales in Tokyo in 1969, featuring an eclectic mix of Western, Japanese and Chinese art. These were followed by further sales in 1970 and in 1980, and the opening of a local office in 1973. When Sotheby's had its first sale in Tokyo, also in 1969, Thompson was dismayed to find out how protected the Japanese market was, says Nicolas Chow, Asia Chairman and Worldwide Head of Asian Art, who joined the house in 1999: 'Auctions were restricted to dealers only, and since they did not welcome foreign competition, the dealers boycotted Sotheby's. So, after one or two sales, Julian decided it was not going to work in Japan.'[13]

The late 1960s and early 1970s, despite episodes of great turmoil, also saw a wealthier Hong Kong increasingly embracing the latest international trends in entertainment, retail and lifestyle. As mentioned in the Introduction, the city's free-port status has always been its trump card. It was, however, untested as an international auctions market and might not have been Thompson's choice for his Asian sales if not for an entrepreneurial, and by all accounts, charismatic businesswoman and socialite called Mamie Howe.[14] Among her many roles at the time, the Shanghai-born and US-educated tastemaker was a senior buyer for Lane Crawford, the upmarket Hong Kong retailer founded in 1850 which had an Asian art and antiques section. She approached Thompson with the idea of a series of joint sales with Lane Crawford, which eventually took place in November 1973 at the Mandarin Hotel in the central business district.[15] London- and Asia-sourced consignments fetched record prices despite the fact that the world was very much in the grip of the 'Oil Shock' of 1973–4. Thompson was so thrilled with the £1 million sales achieved that he immediately decided to set up an office there. Christie's followed with its first Hong Kong sale in

1986, Bonhams in 2007 and Phillips in 2015. The two leading mainland Chinese houses, Poly Auction and China Guardian, began sales in Hong Kong in 2012.

A major turning point came in the early 1990s, when foreign countries lifted most sanctions against China imposed after the 1989 Tiananmen Square crackdown, and the economy soared on strong demand for Chinese exports. The late 1990s also saw the arrival of the first Chinese private museums which, like their counterparts in the rest of the world, are extremely important patrons for both galleries and auction houses alike.[16] Sotheby's Chow remembers William Chak Kin-man, the dealer, coming into the Hong Kong saleroom in 1999 with a new client from Chaozhou, a small provincial city: 'The buyer from Chaozhou bought up a storm.'[17] That was when Chinese buying power began to show itself, he says.

In the early 2000s Sotheby's and Christie's moved all their regular auctions in Asia to Hong Kong, turning the city into the third-biggest auction hub after London and New York, and offering more categories on top of Chinese and Asian antiques and paintings.

Chinese Contemporary Art Fever

From time immemorial, Hong Kong entrepreneurs have looked for opportunities to sell Chinese products to the rest of the world. And so Hong Kong became the first primary market for contemporary Chinese art, thanks to pioneers such as Alisan Fine Arts, founded by Alice King Tung Chee-ping and Sandra Walters in 1981, and Hanart TZ Gallery, founded by the scholarly Johnson Chang Tsong-zung in 1983. Early buyers were mainly Hong Kong's sizeable population of Western expatriates. Later, in the 1990s, a number of Western dealers with a special interest in living Chinese artists moved to Hong Kong – among them, the late Manfred Schoeni from Switzerland and Plum Blossoms Gallery, founded by the American Stephen McGuinness.

A property and stock-market bubble in the early 1990s fuelled the fin-de-siècle party mood ahead of the city's handover to Communist

China. In the end, the 1997 handover did not put the damper on the art market at all. Christie's Hong Kong's sales in November 1996 were the highest since it began operating in the city ten years before, and similarly, Sotheby's sales were up 40 per cent on the previous year. That was also the time when the flamboyant businessman, raconteur and well-connected socialite David Tang Wing-cheung filled the walls of his newly opened China Club with Chinese contemporary art selected by Johnson Chang and became a crucial tastemaker who convinced others that art offered valuable perspectives on the historic changes taking place in China.[18]

In 2004 Sotheby's then Director of the China and Southeast Asia department Henry Howard-Sneyd decided to hold a contemporary Chinese art auction in Hong Kong. Led by their Chinese painting specialist Evelyn Lin (now President of Greater China at Pace Gallery), the Hong Kong sale saw 47 of the 50 lots sold. The following November, Christie's also chose Hong Kong to reboot its Asian contemporary art auction (the first, held in London in 1998, had been a flop). It was a resounding success. The top lot was a painting by Yue Minjun, called *Gweong-Gweong* (1993), which sold for about ten times its estimate to fetch HK$4.9 million (US$641,680). (Just three years later, the same painting was sold again in another Christie's Hong Kong auction for HK$54 million.) Prices kept going up as Chinese art gained more exposure through international exhibitions. In 2007 Yue's haunting *Execution* (1995), which shows a row of laughing men about to be executed in Tiananmen Square, sold for a record £2.9 million (US$5.97 million) at a Sotheby's London auction. The seller was a young British banker who had bought the painting from Schoeni's gallery in On Hing Terrace in 1995 for HK$250,000 (US$32,200).[19]

The boom in contemporary Chinese art was one reason why Hong Kong auctions moved out of the hotel ballrooms where they had been held for decades and into the massive halls of the Hong Kong Convention and Exhibition Centre. From 2005–6 and until 2023, Sotheby's and Christie's held twice-yearly Spring and Autumn flagship sales there, which were spectacles in themselves, featuring previews and sales of watches, handbags, jewellery, Chinese furniture and a variety of fine art categories all under one roof. As we shall see later, in Chapter 5, Western auction houses opened their own purpose-built exhibition and sales rooms after 2023, anticipating another wave of significant growth.

Auction Houses and China

Apart from the city's fundamental attractiveness as a trading port – mainland China charges up to 34 per cent tax on imported art, versus Hong Kong's 0 per cent, for example – Hong Kong was also a major recipient of the massive capital outflow from the mainland. In 2007 China experienced a record 14.2 per cent growth in its GDP. With limited options for investments domestically, capital flowed freely into Hong Kong property, stocks and art.[20] That was the time of indiscriminate speculation, when Chinese collectors' new appetite for their country's own contemporary art sent prices up by 2000 per cent from 2004 to 2008, according to Artnews, making it the fastest-growing segment of the international art market.[21] By 2013 Zeng Fanzhi's *The Last Supper* (2001), the largest of his *Mask* series, commanded the highest price ever paid for a contemporary Asian artist, selling for US$23.3 million during Sotheby's Autumn sales in Hong Kong that marked the house's 40th year in Asia.

The Hong Kong art market reflects the continued existence of the firewall that separates the city and mainland China under the 'one country, two systems' framework outlined in the Introduction. While any auction company can trade without limitation in Hong Kong, foreign auction houses face major restrictions in mainland China, which banned auctions in 1956 and only allowed them again in 1991. For example, they are prohibited from selling any Chinese works of art made in 1949 or before, and are limited when it comes to selling works by foreign artists who died after 1949. This explains the vast discrepancy between Christie's sales volume on the mainland and in Hong Kong. As the only Western auction house to hold regular auctions in mainland China, Christie's sold US$24.5 million in Shanghai in 2023 compared with around US$383 million sold in its Hong Kong Autumn sales alone. Sotheby's opened a new China headquarters in Shanghai in 2023 with online auctions and sales under its 'Buy Now' platform, but no in-person auction yet.

If the mainland market opens up, it would give the international auction houses access to a sizeable, though volatile, market. In 2011, when it peaked, total auction sales of artworks and cultural artefacts in the mainland reached RMB55.4 billion (US$8.6 billion), but by 2022 this had dipped 70 per cent to RMB16.5 billion (US$2.4 billion).[22] Both Sotheby's and Christie's are continuing to lobby for more access. The other Western auction houses in Hong Kong with a consistent presence are Bonhams and Phillips. As the first major auction house that did not sell antiques in Hong Kong, Phillips brought a younger energy to the market with its focus on contemporary art. Its arrival also coincided with a drop in the average age of Asian collectors and growing interest in works by international, living artists.

The Chinese Houses

'One country, two systems' also applies to how mainland China's main auction houses operate in the city. According to Artprice, China Guardian and Poly Auction were the fourth and fifth biggest auction houses in the world in 2023 based on fine art and NFT auction turnover.[23] They began holding auctions in Hong Kong in 2012, focusing on selling consignments sourced from overseas and in Hong Kong. While they have both built up a significant presence in the city, their sales there are dwarfed by their domestic turnovers in Beijing. For example, in 2023, China Guardian recorded total turnover of US$871.3 million (across all categories). Out of that, only US$153 million was sold in Hong Kong.

China's top auction houses continue to have their main market and collectors' network on the mainland and it has taken time to convince their clients to trust their Hong Kong platforms, says Guo Tong, China Guardian's Vice President and Head of the Chinese Paintings and Calligraphy Department. The decision to come to Hong Kong in

2012 was partly driven by the fact that Sotheby's and Christie's were increasing their marketing efforts on the mainland, with the latter launching their first Shanghai sale in 2013. Guo explains: 'We thought, if they could come here, shouldn't we go out? Hong Kong was the most familiar city outside of the mainland so we decided to start there.'[24] The Hong Kong operation, which deals mostly with consigners outside of China, was seen as a 'good training ground for China Guardian to learn to become an international company'.

The Hong Kong Decade

The 21st century has been called the Asian Century because of the region's ascendency economically. For the international art market, the second decade of the 21st century was very much the Hong Kong Decade. While the local art scene had yet to impinge on global awareness, a Hong Kong contemporary art fair that appeared in 2008, just as China unleashed a 4 trillion yuan (US$596 billion) economic stimulus package, soon drew attention to the city's potential. As co-founder Magnus Renfrew told Melanie Gerlis in her 2021 book *The Art Fair Story*, galleries around the world were in the depths of despair during the global financial crisis, but the new Art HK fair still went okay. 'And okay was the new fabulous', he said.[25]

By 2011, things were more than okay. The fair was capturing the explosive growth in Chinese demand for international art and had grown to have 260 galleries from 38 countries participating. That year, Swiss trade fair giant MCH Group bought a 60 per cent stake in Art HK and in 2013 rebranded it as Art Basel Hong Kong, eventually buying out the original founders.[26] As Gerlis writes, the well-oiled machine that is the world's most powerful art-fair franchise helped lure Chinese collecting taste away from homegrown artists and towards Western contemporary and modern art.[27] Quickly, Chinese collectors started to make headlines by buying Western blue-chip art.[28] For example, in 2015, taxi driver-turned-billionaire Liu Yiqian paid US$170.4 million including fees for one of Amedeo Modigliani's reclining nude paintings at a New York auction.[29]

Emboldened by the fair's success and the beginnings of an ambitious cultural quarter in the West Kowloon district, Western galleries began to open in the city's Central business district, then the world's most expensive place to rent a commercial space.[30] The first was Ben Brown, the London dealer, who in 2009 set up his first overseas branch in Pedder Building, a colonial landmark in the heart of Central district. He did have the inside scoop on the Hong Kong buzz since he grew up in Hong Kong and his artist mother Rosamond was then still living in the family's beautiful 'Pink House' on the Peak.[31]

He was soon joined by the biggest and most international dealer of them all. Larry 'Go-Go' Gagosian had decided to go East and, in 2011, opened a lavish space at the top of Pedder Building. The second-hand clothes shops that were Brown's original neighbours were soon displaced by more arrivals: Simon Lee, Lehmann Maupin, Massimo De Carlo, veteran local dealer Johnson Chang's Hanart TZ Gallery, and Pearl Lam Galleries, whose eponymous founder was born in Hong Kong and is as famous for her globetrotting art adventures as her purple hair. Later, local architect and collector William Lim designed a new high-rise in nearby Queen's Road Central especially for art galleries, called H Queen's. Its first tenants after it opened in 2018 included mega dealers David Zwirner, Pace and Hauser & Wirth. The latter moved to a nearby street-level location to expand its public programme in 2024.[32]

The number of homegrown galleries also exploded, partly due to the rise of a new gallery district in Hong Kong's 'Southside' (a stretch of factory buildings in the districts of Wong Chuk Hang and Tin Wan). There, you can find some of the most ambitious and exciting local galleries, such as Blindspot, Empty Gallery and Kiang Malingue – all three regularly participate in major international art fairs and are increasingly placing their artists in institutions and biennales around the world. The enthusiasm for Hong Kong was captured by Renfrew's book on Hong Kong published in 2017. In it, the co-founder of Art HK described a city which felt like 'neutral territory'. 'There is probably nowhere in the world where so many people feel equally at home', he declared.[33]

3

Art in a Time of Crisis

Seismic Booms

Things were looking good during Art Basel week in March 2018, but even the clinking of champagne glasses and the mwah-mwahs of the jet set could not block out the rumblings of political tectonic shifts. The bonhomie between the two superpowers that safeguarded Hong Kong's position in the world was fracturing. Many events happened in 2018 that soured relations between China and the United States. For example, US President Donald Trump began to impose punishing trade tariffs against China, just as the latter's economic growth had slowed to a 26-year low.[1]

In Hong Kong, local political tension was also mounting, with Chinese officials and nationalist politicians ramping up warnings against foreign interference, as a fringe movement demanding Hong Kong independence began to emerge.[2] But nobody could have imagined that there would be a four-year, complete suspension of normal life that would last from 2019 to 2023.

Art and the 2019 Protests

In February 2019 a gruesome murder committed by a Hong Kong man in Taiwan prompted Carrie Lam, the Hong Kong Chief Executive, to propose a change to the law so as to allow extradition of fugitives wanted by not just Taiwan but also Macau and mainland China. Many Hong Kongers became fearful that such a change would puncture the seal between their robust and independent common-law system and China's less transparent judiciary.[3] While largely peaceful to begin with, violent face-offs between protestors, the police and pro-government counter-protesters grew in number and in scale for around fifteen months from 2019 to 2020. As was seen on television the world over, dramatic scenes emerged on a daily basis as a city known for order, efficiency and safety dissolved into utter chaos. Parts of Hong Kong resembled a war zone. Families were ripped apart as political views polarised. The protests ended soon after mass arrests were made and China bypassed the local legislature and brought in a new national security law on 30 June 2020. Beijing and the Hong Kong administration have blamed the unrest on 'external influences' and foreign powers' efforts to 'oppress China'.[4]

Historically, Hong Kong artists are rarely overtly political (see Chapter 1). But the Hong Kong protest movements of the 21st century, aided by social media, churned out seas of protest art. Apart from the ubiquitous yellow umbrellas, the symbol best remembered from the 2014 Umbrella movement was a monumental paper and wooden sculpture dubbed *Umbrella Man*. The 2019 protests had their giant mascot too – a four-metre tall, crowd-funded, 3D-printed sculpture of a female protestor wearing protective goggles and a gas mask. Protesters (the 'yellows') managed to hoist *Lady Liberty* to the top of Lion Rock Mountain, symbol of Hong Kong's can-do spirit ever since a 1970s television series was named after it. Two days later, the statue with its flag carrying a slogan calling for the city's 'liberation' was found to have been vandalised, presumably by equally agile anti-protestors (the 'blues').[5]

A cat-and-mouse chase between the two camps meant the city saw frequent changeovers of the protestors' mass-produced agitprop. New posters, stickers and sprayed messages would reappear within hours of a wall being cleared by the 'blues'. A nameless army of around two hundred designers used Telegram, a messaging app favoured by protestors, to produce visual propaganda ranging from elaborate paintings and caricatures of politicians to slick infograms about planned protests.

The sheer explosion of art captured the world's attention, with the *Financial Times* describing it as an 'upswell of creativity in a city best known for finance and skyscrapers'.[6] Kacey Wong, Hong Kong's most prominent art activist, was right there in the front line. Wong is a former architect with a Master's degree in sculpture from the Chelsea College of Arts, London, and a doctorate in fine arts from the Royal Melbourne Institute of Technology. His sculptural and performative practice used to be political with a small 'p'. *Paddling Home* (2009), now part of the permanent collection of M+, saw him moving into a micro apartment that floated in the harbour on plastic barrels, a critique of the city's property market as well as a symbol of Hong Kongers' unmoored identity. But after the arrest of artist-activist Ai Weiwei in Beijing in 2011, Wong, an admirer of the Chinese provocateur, became very outspoken against the Chinese Communist Party.[7] He attended protests in costume, often with elaborate props and a team of actors, to ridicule the authorities.[8] In 2019, he would dress up as the Chinese police one day, threatening to drag protestors into a red metal cage, and as Moses the next, reading out the 'Commandments' of the protestors.[9]

A New Chapter in Art History?

Most artists who joined the protests did so more quietly. But away from the protest sites, politics dominated discussions at the many exhibition openings that went ahead during that time. These included the duo of solo exhibitions by two socially engaged artists, Luke Ching Chinwai and South Ho, at local gallery Blindspot on 7 September 2019. Both were showing works that were made before the protests, but they seemed very relevant to what was happening outside.

Ching's section, called *Liquefied Sunshine*, featured a wall of post-cards showing Hong Kong and Taiwan landmarks obscured by white marks mimicking the effects of rain. *Weather Report: Liquefied Sunshine* (2014–15), which includes a dual-channel video, can be seen to question the perceived stability of two places that are as exposed to typhoons and rainstorms as they are to troubles with their giant neighbour. Ho's part of the exhibition was also weather-inspired. His black and white photographs of typhoon-damaged trees in Hong Kong struck many visitors then as symbols of grief and helplessness, underscored by the exhibition title *Force Majeure*.[10]

There were artists who were simply paralysed by the extraordinary events happening. Chow Chun-fai, one of the original Fotanians (see Chapter 2), could not paint for months. He said he still went to his studio every day, but he would just sit there, overcome with doubts about the purpose of art-making when the city was in crisis.[11] He did take photographs of the protests, which he later reproduced on canvases with an orange underpaint to express the intense feelings of the time, describing them as the most emotional paintings he had ever made.[12]

On the whole, art institutions and commercial galleries refrained from siding with either the 'yellows' or the 'blues'. Most respected the fact that many in their sector were sympathetic to concerns about fundamental rights and freedoms raised during the protests, and many did close their doors or allow staff to take the day off on 12 June 2019, when a general strike was called to pressure the government into dropping the extradition bill.[13]

Impact on the Art Market

In 2019 Danqing Li had just moved from Shanghai to Hong Kong. Now running her own consultancy in Hong Kong, she arrived as a senior director of commercial gallery Lévy Gorvy, in charge of opening their first Asia venue at the junction of Ice House Street and Connaught Road Central. It was an enviable location – a large, street-level presence right next to the Mandarin Oriental hotel – or so she thought. The business district saw its share of protest action, and Connaught Road Central was where some of the worst skirmishes happened. With protest roadblocks all over the place and the use of tear gas by riot police just outside, the gallery had to pull down the shutters and restrict access to its inaugural exhibition of Frank Stella's 1970s assemblages.

Li simply carried on, telling me at the time that she worked in the gallery throughout the protests by going in through the back entrance. Business was limited, but with much of the gallery's international secondary sales conducted online or by phone, life went on.[14] Later, the company became Lévy Gorvy Dayan & Wei, having been joined by Rebecca Wei, the former Christie's Asia Chair. The lack of in-person visits by clients eventually saw it closing its physical space in the city during the economic downturn of 2024.[15]

Noah Horowitz, now Chief Executive Officer of Art Basel globally, was a frequent visitor to Hong Kong when he was the fair's Director of Americas. And, speaking in January 2024, he remembers the 2019 fair clearly:

> It wasn't the only moment when there had been protests in Hong Kong over the years, though not at that level, obviously. When the fair happened in March that year the protests were just about happening. So, you know, we have never directly been impacted, not the fair, and not the ability to show anything in the show. A lot of our job is really to share the reality of what things are like on the ground, and that is on an ongoing basis now.[16]

In fact, the 2019 fair, visited by 88,000 people, became a benchmark of normality in subsequent years. Unbeknownst to Hong Kong at the time, a killer virus was making its way to the city, and the fair would not recover to its pre-Covid scale until 2024.[17]

The auction houses' Autumn 2019 sales were more affected by the protests – the Hong Kong Convention and Exhibition Centre is close to the Central Government Compound and therefore smack in the middle of the protest action that was then at its peak. Artnet reported a 6 per cent drop in sales by value in the September to November 2019 period compared with the Autumn sales of 2018, though auction houses cheered the fact that a lack of physical attendance was made up by online and phone biddings – a taste of what was to come next.[18]

The Years of Pandemic Isolation

The first local cases of COVID-19 were detected in late January 2020. In February, Art Basel said it was cancelling the Hong Kong fair that year because of the 'sudden and widespread outbreak'. Some local galleries voiced their objection at the time but that was soon overtaken by events.[19] In March, the world's most open trading hub closed itself off from the rest of the world, including China, by closing border checkpoints, imposing mandatory quarantine for as long as three weeks and, at times, banning entry to non-residents. It did not fully reopen its borders until February 2023, a full year after Singapore did.

Hong Kong had to follow China's 'zero Covid' policy and to prioritise the reopening of its border with the mainland, and so it adopted strict social distancing rules and mandatory hospitalisation for anyone found to have the virus.[20] The system buckled. There were horrific scenes of body bags kept in hospital wards where patients were staying because the mortuaries were overflowing. Mothers were separated from their newborns if one of them caught the virus.[21] The once full streets turned silent. Hong Kong came to have the world's highest COVID-19 death rate.[22] Many sectors of the economy went into freefall,[23] and the mental toll on a community that had yet to recover from the recent political turmoil was enormous.[24]

But the art scene, if anything, became more determined, more united and, for some businesses, more profitable. It helped that Hong Kong never had a city-wide lockdown so people could go out, just not in groups. As soon as the borders were shut, local galleries, institutions, auction houses and public relations firms rallied together and launched the ART Power HK campaign to keep locals abreast of in-person exhibitions and other art events that were still running.[25]

In June 2020, Hong Kong Art Gallery Association members staged their own art fair in Tai Kwun to replace the cancelled Art Basel and the satellite fair Art Central. The response by local collectors was so encouraging that Art Basel decided to hold a small edition with 22 galleries in November 2020, jointly with local fair Fine Art Asia, and then relaunched the regular fair in spring 2021 using a hybrid model that allowed overseas galleries to participate remotely. There were even new businesses and non-profits that appeared during an otherwise difficult period, helmed by passionate individuals. For example, Eunice Tsang, a prescient and inspired curator, set up the non-profit art space Current Plans in the working-class neighbourhood of Sham Shui Po in 2021. Around the same time, artists Jeremy Ip and Daniel Stempfer separately opened their own non-profits, Wure Area and Feyerabend respectively, in similarly unglamorous parts of Kowloon.

On the commercial side, father and son Dominique and Arthur de Villepin opened a gallery in Hong Kong in 2019, right in the middle of the protests. Arthur has lived in the city since 2010 and his father, a former French prime minister, has been deeply involved in the art world since his early career as a diplomat. The gallery, set up as a French 'maison', is known for exquisitely presented exhibitions of a broad range of both modern and contemporary art. Married couple Willem Molesworth and Ysabelle Cheung set up PHD Group in 2021, a gallery inside a quirky, rooftop space once used by Cheung's grandfather as a private clubhouse. The young entrepreneurs set up their first business together to give more visibility to women, Queer and other under-represented artists.

In 2022 Art Intelligence Global, the high-end art consultancy founded by former Sotheby's rainmakers Amy Cappellazzo and Yuki Terase, opened an exhibition space in Hong Kong. Exhibitions include solo presentations of Jeff Koons, Gerhard Richter and a group show of female Abstract Expressionists. There were also new galleries offering more accessible styles of art, often inspired by street art, Pop art and anime, which tapped into a surge of interest in art collecting during the pandemic when people were spending far more time at home.

As artists and curators hunkered down and continued to exhibit, it was striking how important the arts came to be for many people during that time. Non-profits and commercial galleries reported far greater footfall than ever before. It was more than just a matter of having a captive audience. Contemporary art provided an important space for recent traumas to be processed and for a shattered community to be rebuilt. Among the many memorable pandemic-era exhibitions was *Can't Touch This!*, a group show at WMA Space that was facilitated by artist Angela Su, having started out as a book project by writer Chloe Lai, founder of book-sharing space Nose in the Books. The show began with Siu Wai Hang's *Hot Shots* (2021), a miniature cemetery made up of dozens of headshots taken with a thermal camera – like the ones that were ubiquitous in public areas during the pandemic. And it finished full circle with Kenji Wong Wai-kin's *When I look at you right now …* (2021), built around readings by young parents like himself in Hong Kong, both giddy with excitement and agonising about the future.[26]

Luke Ching had a prolific pandemic. He had a solo exhibition at Para Site in 2020 called *Glitch in the Matrix*, a humorous and humanistic response to the changes taking place in society, and participated in a group show of five Hong Kong artists in the 2021 Helsinki Biennale. Meanwhile, he was out campaigning for better treatment of cleaners working for the Mass Transit Railway system during the pandemic, by becoming one himself.

There were even the rare international artists who visited. Tobias Berger, Tai Kwun's Head of Art at the time, managed to convince Francis Alÿs and Pipilotti Rist to put up with weeks of quarantine in 2020 and 2022 respectively for their first solo exhibitions in the city, to the delight of the local art community. Alÿs made a new work, called *Prohibited Steps*, during his fortnight of isolation on Lamma Island (when home quarantines were still allowed). The short video of him walking blindfolded near the edges of the flat rooftop captured the way everyone was similarly spooked by what was happening.

Galleries, whether locally owned or not, focused more on Hong Kong art because international shipping had become nigh-impossible and extremely expensive due to strict testing and quarantine rules for crew members. The result was greater visibility for different generations of local artists and, for some, like Jaffa Lam, career breakthroughs.

Generally, both private dealers and auction houses enjoyed record sales despite the sombre mood in the city, defying the broader economic downturn. New auction records were set in 2021 and 2022: Hong Kong-born Firenze Lai's *Weight* (2013) was sold for just over US$637,000 including fees at Christie's in May. The buyer was from Hong Kong and the sale showed that collectors were increasingly of the view that Hong Kong art, after years of being overlooked, was underpriced compared with mainland Chinese art, said Evelyn Lin, then the Co-head of the 20th and 21st century art department for Christie's Asia-Pacific.[27] Modern and contemporary art sales at Sotheby's, Christie's and Phillips had seen combined sales in Hong Kong rising 27 per cent from 2018 to 2019 to US$750 million, according to data supplied by ArtTactic. Sales were flat in 2020, but in 2021 the total climbed a staggering 72 per cent to US$1.3 billion for the year.[28]

China's biggest auction house, Poly Culture, saw its Hong Kong sales jump 52 per cent to US$333 million in the same year while China Guardian more than doubled its sales from US$53 million to US$120 million. China Guardian, like the other Chinese giant Poly Auction, has no immediate plans to expand in Hong Kong, but Vice-President Guo Tong says there is every reason to hope that business will enter a new phase of growth: 'So many rich people left China during the COVID-19 pandemic for Singapore, Hong Kong, Japan, the US. Many of them are our clients. Most of their assets are now in Hong Kong and overseas. So we expect more of them to buy and sell in Hong Kong.'[29] Sales were also lifted by online buying and enormous Asian interest in the ultimate pandemic craze – non-fungible tokens (NFTs). To build up its digital art business in the region, Sotheby's based its New York NFT expert, Max Moore – known for his promotion of the Bored Ape Yacht Club NFTs – in Hong Kong from 2021 to 2024.[30] And a local fair called the Digital Art Fair was also launched that year.

The resilience of the market prompted Christie's to announce in the summer of 2021 that it had signed a ten-year lease on a new Asia Pacific headquarters in a new building designed by Zaha Hadid Architects that will allow it to hold year-round auctions and private sales from 2024. Christie's CEO Guillaume Cerutti explained:

> We were brave to announce it at a moment of uncertainty. It's because we really believe in all the advantages of doing business here and because the art ecosystem is already present. That's the first aspect. The second aspect is that we are part of this ecosystem, so if we make this choice, that sends a signal to others. And they will think, well, if Christie's is doing this then we will stay as well.[31]

Not everyone stayed. South Korea's Seoul Auction, a top house in a country that saw its art star rising during the pandemic, abandoned its Hong Kong exhibition space in 2020. New York-headquartered Lehmann Maupin, which opened its first Asia gallery in Pedder Building in 2013, also closed the Hong Kong space in 2020 after it opened a larger space, in Seoul.

The Exodus

The art community did itself proud by holding it all together between 2019 and 2023, but Hong Kong was bleeding talent and competitiveness. Other cities used their head start in the post-pandemic recovery to attract art-market players. Seoul became a magnet for international galleries and was picked by Frieze, Art Basel's main art-fair rival, to launch its first Asia fair in 2022. In January 2023 Magnus Renfrew and his partners launched Art SG in Singapore, the city Hong Kong is most often compared with and an increasingly popular place for wealthy Chinese and Southeast Asian families to park their wealth.[32] Describing Singapore, Renfrew reused a phrase he once applied to Hong Kong: 'It is regarded as "neutral territory" and there is probably nowhere in the world where everyone feels so equally at home', he said, implying that Hong Kong's reputation for openness has been overtaken.[33]

Expatriates and locals alike left in droves, with hundreds of thousands moving abroad citing COVID-19 restrictions as well as fears regarding the Hong Kong way of life and its freedoms after Beijing introduced a national security law in 2020 to restore order and project its authority in the city.[34] While Beijing maintained that Hong Kong would retain key freedoms, the new national security regime is accompanied by a vigorous campaign to instil Chinese nationalism and patriotism in Hong Kong, as well as new election rules that disqualify opposition voices deemed unpatriotic.[35] There are concerns over the new rules' impact on freedom of expression, which will be further examined in Chapter 5, and many artists, curators, art writers and museum specialists have left as a result.

Artists who have left include those whose practices are the most attached to local Hong Kong society and identity, and their departures have stirred great sadness as well as leaving a major hole in the city's art scene. Lam Tung-pang, founding member of the Fotanians, overcame his fear of flying to move to Vancouver in 2022, and the politically outspoken Kacey Wong has moved to Taiwan. But the United Kingdom has been the most popular destination for locals after the British government created a new immigration route for Hong Kong citizens in 2020. Based on data provided by the UK Home Office, around 150,400 people left for Britain under the bespoke migration pathway from 2021 to 2024.[36] Two Hong Kong artists who have seen their works break through the HK$1 million mark in auctions are in London now: Chris Huen Sin-kan and Firenze Lai Ching-yin. The political cartoonist Justin Wong Chiu-tat and his wife Stella Fong Wing-yan, former head of learning at M+, are also in London. C&G Artpartment's husband-and-wife duo, Gum Cheng and Clara Cheung, are in Sheffield. There are many, many more.

4

M+: Hong Kong's Global Museum

Hong Kong's dramatic skyline has a lot going on at night: the sea of illuminated skyscrapers that outlines the dense urban centre built on either side of Victoria harbour, and the waterfront that comes to life in a nightly sound and laser show. But nothing quite catches the eye like the M+ museum located on the Kowloon waterfront. The inverted T-shape building with a flat base and a central, vertical plank, designed by Herzog & de Meuron, has a 110-metre-wide, harbour-facing facade that turns into a giant cinema screen every evening. Cleverly embedded with 5500 LED lights, the glass and Italian terracotta tiles become a constantly changing display of commissioned films, exhibition advertisements and, once, an interactive video game that you could connect to from your phone.

Even without this conspicuous feature, M+, which opened its doors in 2021, would still be the most watched symbol of how a new Hong Kong is attempting to project its cultural ambition while grappling with new national security laws and the government's desire to cultivate a nationalistic cultural identity. That sometimes slightly quizzical interest has only increased as wider questions have arisen over whether a progressive and international cultural institution still has a place in Hong Kong today.

A Focus on Now

In 1998 the first government of the newly established Hong Kong Special Administrative Region announced a plan to build state-of-the-art cultural venues on reclaimed land near the colonial-era Tsim Sha Tsui cultural complex.[1] Plenty has been said about the early years of the project, as the government hummed and hawed before dismantling an unpopular idea of a completely canopied district built and operated by private developers, adopting the current unshielded, largely publicly funded model which nevertheless has its own problems.[2]

The original Build-Operate-Transfer option would likely have resulted in a museum franchise – or two. Both the Guggenheim and Centre Pompidou were in discussion with a consortium of developers.[3] There was public disappointment at the time when it became clear that Hong Kong would not get a 'brand name' institution. In hindsight, it was a powerful postcolonial gesture of cultural independence when Hong Kong chose instead to build a new kind of museum in its own image. The problem, however, is that Hong Kong's image of itself is fractured and contested.

In 2006, just after the private developers' model was dropped, the government appointed local specialists to a Museum Advisory Group (MAG). An early plan for a cluster of four separate themed museums was quickly abandoned over concerns about costs, and replaced by the group's singularly bold and progressive proposal: one world-class museum called M+, short for Museum Plus, that would focus on a 'broadly defined' range of 20th and 21st-century visual culture. It would have a 'Hong Kong perspective', a global vision and a focus on 'the now', which eliminates the unhelpful differentiation between 'modern' and 'contemporary'. To begin with, it should cover design, moving image, popular culture and visual art.[4]

The Beginning

There were existing museums around the world embracing a multi-disciplinary approach, such as the Centre Pompidou in Paris, the V&A

in London and New York's Museum of Modern Art (MoMA).[5] But M+ – which has stunning views of the harbour outside, sweeping ampitheatres inside and out, and an exceptional members' lounge filled with local art donated by Hong Kong architect William Lim – was the first 'museum of visual culture' to be built from the ground up in Asia, the plus sign an indication of the breadth of its collection and programmes.

The hiring in 2011 of Lars Nittve as the museum's first Executive Director was widely seen as a first step towards the building of a world-class museum. Nittve was the founding Director of the much-praised Tate Modern in London, which had opened in 2000 in a former power station converted by Herzog & de Meuron. He also helped transform Moderna Museet in his home country, Sweden, again to wide acclaim. Tobias Berger, the German-born veteran curator who ran local non-profit Para Site from 2005 to 2008, was hired shortly after as Curator of Visual Art, further setting M+ apart from existing local museums mostly run by ethnic Chinese civil servants.

The first priority was to start filling the future museum – one of the biggest contemporary museums in the world, with 65,000 m^2 total floor area, 33 galleries, 17,000 m^2 of exhibition space, nearly 6000 m^2 of conservation and storage facility on site, and three cinemas.

The Sigg Collection

In 2011 Nittve and Jane DeBevoise on the Museum Advisory Group heard that Uli Sigg, the businessman and former Swiss ambassador to China, was looking to give away his vast collection of contemporary Chinese art to a Chinese museum. (DeBevoise is a former Deputy Director of the Guggenheim Museum in New York and Chair of the Asia Art Archive in Hong Kong.)

Sigg, who was born in 1946, was travelling regularly to mainland China within years of the country opening up in 1979 and soon started visiting fledgling communities of experimental artists as an alternative way for him to understand Chinese society.[6] He made the early decision to build what he calls an 'encyclopaedic' and 'impersonal' collection that mirrored the unpredictable and dramatic transformation in the world's most populous country since the Cultural Revolution. Apart from major movements such as Political Pop and Cynical Realism, it is also rich in conceptual installations, photography and video, and includes examples of academic paintings in the official Socialist Realist style.

The case was put to Sigg by Nittve, DeBevoise and the Chairman of the West Kowloon Cultural District Authority (WKCDA), Henry Tang, that M+ was the best museum for the collection because it had curatorial freedom and international reach that mainland institutions lacked. In 2012 Sigg agreed to donate 1464 works, then valued at HK\$1.3 billion (US\$163 million), and sold an additional 47 pieces to the future museum for HK\$177 million. The now renamed M+ Sigg Collection spans the four decades between 1972 and 2012, ending in the year the agreement with the museum was reached. There are gaps. As Sigg has pointed out, there is a gender imbalance because women artists were less visible in the late 20th century.[7] It is also focused on art produced within mainland China rather than what Chinese artists were doing in the rest of the world, including in Hong Kong.[8] But with over 1500 pieces by around 320 artists, it was certainly a way for a new museum to gain a cornerstone collection in one fell swoop, especially after the rise in prices of contemporary Chinese art. The MM Chinese Art Contemporary Index, which tracks prices of art made by Chinese artists born after 1911, rose from 1 in 2001 to 12 in 2011, and peaked at 21.7 in 2020.[9]

Even in 2012, when Hong Kong could genuinely claim to be one of the world's freest artistic environments, museum insiders say that there were early discussions with regards to how best to protect a collection which, as the best contemporary art often does, invites critical questions about recent history. The Sigg Collection features many works that simply would not be allowed in mainland China, such as Wang Guangyi's *Mao Zedong: Red Grid No.2* (1989), a portrait of the late Chairman Mao placed behind red bars; Wang Xingwei's *New Beijing* (2001), a painting based on a famous photograph taken during the 1989 Tiananmen Square crackdown; or Ai Weiwei's *Study of Perspective:*

Tian'anmen (1997), a photograph of the artist sticking up his middle finger at the traditional symbol of power in China (more on that later).

The contract between Sigg and the museum ensures that the collection stays visible: three rotations in dedicated galleries over the first few years after opening; a minimum of 5000 m^2 to display the collection during that time; and a percentage of the collection has to be on display at all times, not just in M+ but anywhere in the world. M+ also took the Chinese Contemporary Art Awards, founded by Sigg in 1998, and renamed them The Sigg Prize.

A Global Collection Rooted in Asia

The visionary Nittve laid a solid foundation for the ambitious institution and stepped down in 2016, frustrated by long construction delays at the museum, originally slated for a 2017 opening.[10] The board of the West Kowloon Cultural District Authority, then headed by future Chief Executive Carrie Lam, chose a successor with an equally international CV: Sri Lankan-born Australian Suhanya Raffel. From 1994 to 2013 Raffel was at the Queensland Art Gallery / Gallery of Modern Art (QAGOMA) in Brisbane, where she led its flagship Asia Pacific Triennial of Contemporary Art and rose up to be Acting Director. She then became Deputy Director and Director of Collections at the Art Gallery of New South Wales in Sydney. Having joined M+ in 2016 as Executive Director, and becoming Museum Director in 2019, Raffel oversees a permanent collection defined by the museum as 'rooted in Asia but defined, developed, and examined from a global perspective'.[11]

As mandated by the museum's founding principle, the collection extends far beyond the realm of visual arts to include moving images, architecture, fashion and design. By 2021, when the museum finally opened, a significant 23 per cent of the entire collection was by Hong Kong makers, comprising around 1820 works. In total, there are now over 7000 items dated from 1895 to the present, largely by Asian creators but also by non-Asians whose legacies are felt strongly, including Marcel Duchamp (whose readymades inspired Chinese artists such as Ai Weiwei). Ikko Yokoyama, the Japanese design and architecture curator whose second language is Swedish, says M+ embodies the cosmopolitanism of Hong Kong and is the only institution where an anti-Euro-American-centric viewpoint can develop without resorting to the nationalistic approaches of museums in places such as Japan and Korea: 'Our approach is not binary. We do not present a juxtaposition of Western design history against modern-day China. Our lives have many parallels. It's not just West and East', she told me in 2021.[12]

When Raffel arrived in Hong Kong in 2016, the timetable was to open the museum within three years. With the Sigg Collection already in place, she focused on adding more works by women and from South and Southeast Asia.[13] Like her predecessor, Raffel does not speak Cantonese or Mandarin, but that is not considered an impediment inside an international institution and in the city's contemporary art ecosystem where English is commonly used. 'We have 26 nationalities and 16 different language capacities. M+ can only happen in Hong Kong, because Hong Kong is global, outward, connected and a city open to ideas', she says.[14]

Global Versus Local

Well before the recent nationalistic attacks on M+, which we will come to shortly, the museum's international leadership was sometimes seen as a weakness rather than strength by the local art community. The reputations of Nittve and Raffel, and the diverse experience of those in senior positions, such as Deputy Director Doryun Chong (ex MoMA, New York and Walker Art Center, Minneapolis), can undoubtedly be credited for how enthusiastically M+ is received overseas. But its relationship with the mostly Cantonese-speaking, ethnic Chinese local artistic community in the city has often been fraught.

Back in 2012 the Hong Kong Arts Development Council, which has been presenting a Hong Kong exhibition at the Venice Art Biennale since 2001 (four years before China set up its national pavilion), announced that it had asked M+ and Nittve, then newly arrived as Executive Director, to be in charge of the Venice exhibition. Local artists and curators promptly launched a protest against what they saw as an undemocratic 'black-box operation', as previous participation in Venice was by an open call. It is beyond the scope of this book to discuss the significance of Hong Kong's representation at the Venice Biennale. Suffice to say that, like Hong Kong still having its own Olympics team, the city's participation as a collateral exhibition continues to present its own artistic tradition to the world. Unlike most regional pavilions, the Hong Kong exhibition in Venice has also featured non-Chinese artists. But in 2012 a broader issue was how M+ was deemed to be a well-funded hegemony that marked a major step backward for the public right of participation in the city's artistic development, the curator Jaspar Lau Kin-wah wrote.[15] Today, criticisms have continued about the museum's preference for hiring from overseas to fill its most senior jobs.

A New Kind of Museum

For sure, M+ has a far more international staff than government museums run by local civil servants. As researcher and curator Anqi Li writes in her paper titled 'Bilbao Effect 2.0: The Making of M+', the governance and finance model of M+ is designed to distinguish it from the bureaucratic Leisure and Cultural Services Department museums, in the hope that it can become a dynamic cultural landmark that can contribute to the economic revitalisation of the city, like the Guggenheim Museum Bilbao.[16]

With regards to funding, both M+ and its neighbour in the West Kowloon Cultural District, the Hong Kong Palace Museum, have to actively court patrons and corporate sponsorships like no public museum has done, since the one-off HK$21.6 billion government endowment for the district is expected to run out in 2025. Patrons also sit on three acquisition councils that rigorously vet additions to the collection. Additionally, the museums charge far more for exhibition tickets than existing museums run by the government (general admission at M+ is HK$120).

It was gratifying to M+ that a bold, new rotation of the Sigg Collection, a Yayoi Kusama retrospective exhibition (which subsequently toured to the Guggenheim Museum Bilbao) and a show dedicated to Song Huai-kuei – a fashion icon in China – helped attract 2.8 million visitors in 2023, putting it among the top 20 most-visited art museums in the world, according to *The Art Newspaper*'s annual survey.[17]

The Middle Finger

Even with healthy ticket sales, future funding remains an issue. But it is the political challenges faced by M+ that make it such a closely watched test case for the arts in Hong Kong. In 2021, just seven months before the long-awaited opening of the museum, the Sigg Collection became embroiled in politics and a Sword of Damocles has hung over the museum's head ever since. At the press preview of the completed building on 12 March 2021 Raffel was asked by a journalist if the new National Security Law would stop M+ from exhibiting works by Ai Weiwei, the Chinese artist-activist who was very critical of the Hong Kong government's response to the 2019 Hong Kong protests. The museum would have 'no problem' showing Ai's works, she replied. 'Like any global museum, it is our role to present art in a relevant and appropriate manner and stimulate debate, knowledge and pleasure. A city can only be a welcoming arts hub if it offers an open environment for artists and for different views.'[18]

Such a comment would have been considered unremarkable in the old Hong Kong, when freedom of expression and curatorial independence were sacrosanct. Back in 2016, for example, there was open discussion by M+ curators about whether the museum should collect ephemeral protest art that had been salvaged from the 2014 Umbrella Movement.[19] (In particular, the museum considered whether to collect the *Umbrella Man*, the monumental cardboard icon that was the guardian angel of the makeshift protest camps in Harcourt Road, a person close to the discussion recalls. It was not considered viable as it was not in good material condition, was too large and it was unclear whether it fitted in with the museum's artistic criteria.)[20]

But in 2021 the political situation had changed and Raffel's comment did not go down well. Fierce condemnation came from nationalist online bloggers, local lawmakers as well as state-owned Chinese newspapers. Critics trawled through the digital catalogue and latched onto Ai's most incendiary image in the collection – *Study of Perspective: Tian'anmen* – as well as works that feature Chairman Mao in playful irony, such as Wang's *Mao Zedong: Red Grid No.2*, and even portrayals of nudity and Queer identity as evidence that the Sigg Collection, because it had been amassed by a Westerner, was dangerous to national security. There were threats of getting the police involved.[21]

The elected Chairman of the Hong Kong Arts Development Council Visual Arts Group (HKADC), the artist Chan Kam-shing, defended M+ and suggested that some of its critics were simply unfamiliar with art. That earned him the label of a pro-protest 'infiltrator' who supported the use of violent means to disrupt Hong Kong. He stepped down from the HKADC saying he feared for his family's safety.[22] The subsequent months leading up to the opening of the museum on 11 November 2021 saw carefully worded statements issued by the then Hong Kong Chief Executive Carrie Lam and Henry Tang, the founding Chairman of WKCDA from 2008 to 2011 who has remained the Chair since he was reappointed in 2017.

Back in 2021 Lam, who was at the tail end of her troubled term as the city's leader, promised that M+ would be law abiding while adhering to the promise of the WKCDA Ordinance, which states that the authority in charge of the cultural district must 'uphold and encourage freedom of artistic expression and creativity'. But the museum was seen to bow to political pressure when, within months of its opening, it removed several controversial images from the first Sigg Collection exhibition, including *Mao Zedong: Red Grid No.2* and *New Beijing*. M+ insisted, however, that this was part of a normal exhibition rotation rather than a case of self-censorship. Other images which had been picked out by critics were taken down from the M+ online catalogue. After that, the furore gradually subsided.[23]

I think back to my first interview with Raffel early in 2017 and wonder if she could see what was coming. 'Politics is not something that has stopped me for the last 30 years and I don't intend for it to stop me this time', she told me.[24] Her total confidence in the project never slipped, in public at least. But she acknowledges that there have been a few tough moments. Six years later, she noted: 'The whole Hsin Chong thing, when that was happening, that was a low. It was hard because I had changed career to come here. It was a commitment that I was going to see through. And I guess the series of very big [challenges] – the 2019 protests and then the pandemic.'[25] (In 2018 M+ had to terminate its arrangement with Hsin Chong, its main building contractor, on grounds of insolvency and poor performance, an extremely messy affair with claims that have yet to be sorted out.) True to her earlier words, Raffel says she was unruffled by the political drama. 'A lot of that was like lancing a wound. It needed to be opened up and allowed out. I think it was really good to work through all that and to ensure the integrity of M+'s curatorial vision was intact.'

It is worth noting that there were politicians who called for the de-accessioning of works deemed to be in violation of the national security law. Individuals close to M+ privately expressed at the time that it was a good thing that M Plus Collections Limited was established in 2016. The museum cannot unilaterally get rid of works in the collection and has to go through the process of an audit by a M+ Collections Board.[26]

The Opening

When M+ finally opened, there was no official launch party. Everyone still had their Covid masks on. And it was a completely domestic affair because the borders were still shut. But nobody who attended the 11 November 2021 event will ever forget it. Finally, we got to see the Sigg Galleries, opening in that first iteration with Wen Pulin's documentary of the seminal 1989 *Chinese Avant-garde Art Exhibition* in Beijing, projected onto a giant screen as such an important piece of history deserved. I remember how myself and fellow journalists noted the presence of several works by Ai Weiwei (though not *Study of Perspective*) as well as works such as Wang Guangyi's *Mao Zedong: Red Grid No.2*, which features the Chairman with a red grid over his portrait. Another major highlight was the design gallery, a witty juxtapositioning of objects from different parts of the world, including an entire sushi restaurant by Japanese designer Kuramata Shiro that local lawmakers had criticised M+ for buying several years previously.

For members of the museum team who had worked intensely, and continued to do so through the protests and the pandemic, it was all suddenly worth it. Isabella Tam, Curator of Visual Art at the museum, says: 'At the opening I was particularly touched to see the first group of families walking into the building. They activated this space, and to me it was the image that I was so grateful to witness.'[27] A former member of the museum staff remembers the pandemic-restricted outdoor 'party' for employees only. Given the emotion of seeing the museum finally open, 'everyone got super wasted', she remembers.[28]

Yeewan Koon, Chair of the Department of Art History at the University of Hong Kong, made a trenchant observation in her 2022 paper on M+, pointing out that the opening exhibition on Hong Kong art made no mention at all of the political upheavals in Hong Kong in recent years. The absence of art that addresses social and political changes after 2014 made the exhibition titled *Here and Beyond* an exercise in nostalgia, she wrote. It could add to criticism among local practitioners that the museum has too little to do with Hong Kong, or is *lei dei*, Cantonese slang for being detached from reality:

> But being *lei dei* also opens a space, willfully or otherwise, where denials and ambiguity allow for a degree of non-accountability. M+'s mission of being a global museum in Asia allows it to produce exhibitions that do not conform to an authorised history of nation-building, but it also allows it to skirt the politics of resistance on the ground. Whether this harms or protects artists and art institutions in the long term remains debatable.[29]

The big international opening party had to wait until 21 March 2023, which was during Art Basel week. Thousands of guests filled the vast Main Hall of the museum and spilled into the harbour-facing terrace where there was music and performances. It was the first time international visitors, including Lars Nittve and his architect wife Shideh Shaygan, saw the completed museum and the mood was that of a long-separated community reunited at last. Raffel says: 'When we opened, the people of Hong

Kong recognised that this was done with integrity. And now the world is recognising it. We all feel very, very proud. And I have to say, I feel it's the best work that I've done in my career. And that's very sustaining.'[30]

Maria Balshaw, Director of the Tate in the UK and long-time advisor to the museum, dismisses concerns that Hong Kong's declining freedoms have curtailed the museum's ambitions: 'M+ is everything I hoped for. Cultural organisations all over the world are under increasing scrutiny by the public as well as by governments. There is intense debate over what is chosen to be shown in museums. And I think the most powerful [way] we can think about it is to say it's because museums matter.'[31]

But yet another crisis is looming. On 18 August 2023 Tang, the WKCDA Chairman, said money was draining from the cultural district like 'rivers of blood'; in the spring of 2024 he warned again that there would soon be no more cash left to commission new exhibitions, and that both M+ and the Hong Kong Palace Museum might have to have more closing days to save costs. The Authority has yet to reveal how much M+ cost to build, as outstanding claims by sub-contractors have not been settled.[32] It has admitted that construction costs have exceeded its original HK\$5.9 billion (US\$760 million) budget. At the time of writing, the government has just allowed WKCDA to raise funds by selling land parcels within the district for residential development. However, the first sale is not expected before 2026, which means that the district will continue to be under financial pressure in the near future.[33]

There are many issues facing the museum going forward. Can it convince the people of Hong Kong and the international community that it has an independent and global vision? Can it adhere to its unique, cosmopolitan founding principle in an increasingly nationalistic world? And what are the new key performance indicators (KPIs) that the government is demanding for further public financial support?[34] A lot is at stake, and the museum's importance goes beyond its role in Hong Kong's cultural ecosystem. When existing ways of understanding the world have led us to a point where humankind seem collectively embroiled in dangerous confrontations, M+'s founding mission to project new perspectives from a city in between great powers now seems all the more urgent.

5

The New Hong Kong

Often described as the most powerful leader of China since Mao Zedong, President Xi Jinping commented on Hong Kong's National Security Law (NSL) when he oversaw the swearing-in of former police officer John Lee Ka-chiu as the city's new Chief Executive: the new law introduced in 2020 had 'pushed Hong Kong from chaos to governance, and into a new stage of moving from governance to prosperity'.[1] As is often the case with Xi's remarks, the phrase became a slogan frequently invoked by officials, and Lee's administration further convinced the new 'patriots-only' legislature to expedite the passing of 'Article 23' in March 2024, a wide-ranging law with heavy penalties for 'incitement to mutiny and disaffection', 'acts with seditious intention' and 'foreign interference', among other things.

Many of Hong Kong's main business partners in the West have condemned the new laws and claimed that they have reduced the city's attractiveness as an international business hub. In return, Beijing and Hong Kong have accused the US, the EU, UK and Canada of 'slandering, smearing and interfering in Hong Kong affairs'.[2]

New Laws for Art

In 2021 *The Pillar of Shame* was seized by the police. The eight-metre sculpture, created by Danish artist Jens Galschiøt in 1997, was later used as evidence for a national security case against the organisers of Hong Kong's annual public vigil for victims of the 1989 Tiananmen Square crackdown.[3] The bright orange pillar depicting 50 writhing, damaged and distorted bodies was once among Hong Kong's best-known pieces of public art. For 24 years it stood on the campus of the University of Hong Kong, after initially being displayed in the candlelight vigils at Victoria Park that were held on 4 June every year to commemorate those who died in 1989.

In 2023 a mural outside a fast-food restaurant featuring caricatures of construction workers wearing standard yellow safety helmets was covered up. According to the owner, the mural was over a decade old and had been created in honour of the builders who frequented the cafe for its affordable meat and rice dishes. But he was warned that it might have violated the NSL because yellow helmets were worn by protesters in 2019. Reluctantly, he signed an agreement allowing the government's Home Affairs Bureau to paint over it.[4]

Apart from the NSL, art practitioners in Hong Kong need to be aware of legal changes brought in through new clauses in existing ordinances, such as the 2021 amendments to the Film Censorship Ordinance and the addition of a national security clause to applications for a Places of Public Entertainment (PPE) Licence or Temporary Places of Public Entertainment (TPPE) Licence. There was ambiguity in the way PPE or TPPE licences were administered before the NSL. Many galleries and other cultural venues are located in factory buildings which, as explained in Chapter 2, have long provided relatively affordable spaces for artists to work in. Technically, any exhibition in Hong Kong requires a TPPE licence in advance. But as bureaucratic logic would have it, events held inside factory buildings are denied TPPE licences because of zoning laws. With the extra national security clause now added, independent and commercial venues are concerned that, if strictly implemented, the licence requirement would make it difficult, if not impossible, for them to survive. Major public venues have always applied for the licences (only venues administered by the government's Leisure and Cultural Services Department are exempt) and, privately, administrators say they worry about where today's national security red lines lie. 'It is this kind of ambiguity that is stifling the arts in Hong Kong', one arts administrator says.[5]

Art Basel Hong Kong confirms that it needs to apply for a TPPE Licence (as do all art fairs). So, technically, such a licence can now be denied if art on sale is found to 'constitute or is likely to cause the occurrence of an offence endangering national security under the National Security Law or other laws of the HKSAR'. Ahead of the fair's 2024 edition in March 2024, Art Basel Hong Kong issued a statement saying: 'At this stage we have no indication that Article 23 will have an impact on the way we operate. We have never faced any censorship issues at our shows, nor have we been asked to do anything differently since the introduction of the National Security Law in 2020.'[6]

Since 2021, there have been periodic reports of exhibitions in independent venues being shut down for operating public events without a TPPE licence. For example, it has happened to Parallel Space, one of a number of original and resourceful independent art spaces that have transformed Sham Shui Po from Hong Kong's poorest neighbourhood into its coolest.[7] Commercial galleries have never been required to have such a licence in the past, which was why there was momentary panic and disbelief in 2021, shortly after the NSL was introduced, when officials from the Food and Environmental Hygiene Department made unannounced visits to four well-established galleries and accused them of having exhibitions without a TPPE licence. The galleries involved later put it down to a 'misunderstanding' and the matter was put to one side. 'We are retailers. When we have openings, they are for invited guests only and not open to the public. So we should be exempt', said one of the gallerists in private.[8]

It has not so far been possible to get clarification on the matter from the Food and Environmental Hygiene Department, which issues the

TPPE licences in consultation with other relevant government departments. In reply to yes/no questions regarding whether exhibitions generally are checked for content that poses a threat to national security, the department simply replied with a copied-and-pasted section of the 'Places of Public Entertainment Ordinance', without further comment.

New Role for Film Censors

To date, film is the only category that has to go through an official vetting process. It should be noted that political censorship of films in British Hong Kong began early in the 20th century and many films were banned on grounds of hurting relations with China. That changed in 1994 when the 'good relations' clause was dropped from the Film Censorship Ordinance on grounds of freedom of expression – a move that angered China at the time.[9] The 2021 NSL clause added to the ordinance, which covers any video work shown in public art exhibitions (but not those sold in galleries), means that censors who were previously only asked to ban or give age ratings based on content 'which portrays, depicts or treats cruelty, torture, violence, crime, horror, disability, sexuality or indecent or offensive language or behaviour', now need to check for content which may encourage, incite and glorify any activities endangering national security.[10] Films, or film titles, that used to be acceptable no longer are. One incident bordering on black humour occurred at M+ in January 2024. Because the film board would not approve M+'s screening of the 1993 classic movie *Beijing Bastards* by Chinese director Zhang Yuan (although the film had nothing to do with politics), M+ removed the title from all of its publicity material as well as from the film's opening sequence, replacing it with 'A Film by Zhang Yuan'.[11]

In February 2023 conceptual artist Florence Lee withdrew her animated film *Elephant in Castle* from a public screening organised by the IFVA Independent Short Film and Video Media Festival in Hong Kong after the film board demanded she made cuts to her dialogue-free, five-minute work that obliquely captures the sadness of

Hong Kong in 2019–20. Lee put the full version online instead.[12] At the time of writing, films that do not get approved by the Film Censorship Board can be accessed online in the city given its still-free access to the internet, including Western social media platforms that are banned on the mainland, with the exception of China-owned TikTok.

Major Source of Art Funding Affected

National security clauses have been added to every government contract since 2022, including the Hong Kong Arts Development Council funding agreements, as well as public and private venue hire agreements. In August 2023 the new minister in charge of culture announced that under the HKADC's peer-review system for funding applications, examiners should judge projects based on national-security criteria.[13] Some artists are saying privately that they no longer dare apply for HKADC funding because of the new national security clause. It states that funding would have to be returned, with interest, if the recipient (or any of its board members, staff, partners, employees, agents, contractors or subcontractors) is or was once engaged in any activities that may harm or be unfavourable to national security. In one of the first publicised examples of a fund recipient being told to return money, the council made it clear that it was simply 'minimising the risk' of the NSL being broken rather than having actual proof that someone had broken the law.[14]

To walk away from HKADC funding is no easy choice. As culture critic Kuh Fei points out, many small- and medium-sized arts groups depend on HKADC funding for up to 90 per cent of their running costs. In 2022–3, the HKADC gave total funding of HK$100.5 million, including annual grants to 50 arts groups and project grants to 286 projects.[15]

Self-censorship

A new term entered into circulation in Hong Kong in 2021. Chief Executive John Lee, former Deputy Commissioner of Police, and the

Secretary for Security Chris Tang, former Commissioner of Police, began warning against 'soft resistance'. They vowed to act against anti-China ideologies 'infiltrating via the media, culture and arts' which can 'poison young people's minds'.[16] Given such warnings, as well as the vague nature of legal red lines, self-censorship in what used to be one of the freest cities in Asia is now common. There are certainly things that artists and curators must avoid in Hong Kong after a series of court rulings since 2020: any message that might be seen as promoting Hong Kong independence;[17] any anti-Beijing protest slogan;[18] playing the protest anthem 'Glory to Hong Kong';[19] and anything that may be construed as encouraging others to commemorate the 4 June anniversary of the Tiananmen Square crackdown.[20]

Rather insidiously, it is now common for the government or individual venues to receive tip-offs, which can be done anonymously using the National Security Department Reporting Hotline set up by the police in 2020. Such complaints have been made regarding the alleged political views of participants in the cultural sector, and venues have been known to cancel shows after being informed that complaints have been lodged. Those affected are often frustrated by the lack of transparency and any appeal mechanism.[21] It has been said that political background checks are conducted surreptitiously and institutions are also warned by third parties not to work with certain people. The immigration department has also denied visit visas and work permits to foreign passport holders suspected of being supportive of the protest movement. The department never confirms reasons for denying entry, but individuals affected have sometimes gone public about their experiences.[22]

State-run Art?

For years, practitioners such as Danny Yung, the influential co-founder of experimental theatre Zuni Icosahedron, had lobbied for a more hands-on cultural policy from the government, which initially inherited the 'small government' approach from the British.[23] Hong Kong culture needed vision and long-term planning, he said. Yung got his wish. In 2021 Hong Kong's cultural development was enveloped into Beijing's national strategy for the first time. The central government's 14th five-year national plan, which covers the period 2021 to 2025, handed Hong Kong a list of detailed missions, including designating the city as a national cultural exchange centre.[24]

New national organisations began to appear in Hong Kong soon after the 2019 protests, with an official mandate to boost China's soft power and encourage Hong Kong's rebellious youth to feel a sense of national belonging. First, there was Bauhinia Culture, a company set up in 2019 by the Chinese government's Ministry of Finance with dual headquarters in Hong Kong and Shenzhen, the technology and finance hub just across the border. The state-owned company consolidated the ownership of around HK$1 billion worth of cultural assets including the China Arts and Entertainment Group (CAEG), which owns major performance venues such as the Guangzhou Opera House and is responsible for the China Pavilion in the Venice Biennale.[25] It also owns Hong Kong-based book publishers, a film company, magazines and is the controlling shareholder of Phoenix Television, a Chinese-language satellite station based in Hong Kong. Headed by a former propaganda chief for the Chinese Communist Party, the low-profile company does not have a website. So far activities directly presented by the Bauhinia Group in Hong Kong have ranged from a 2023 television series promoting the heroism of the Hong Kong police force to CAEG's presentation of the National Ballet of China's performance in Hong Kong in 2024.

In 2020 the Hong Kong branch of the China Federation of Literary and Art Circles, a national association of writers and artists led by the Chinese Communist Party, was inaugurated. Its founders were local practitioners who were already members of the national association and intent on promoting Chinese culture in Hong Kong and helping local artists reach a larger audience on the mainland. It has also been involved in the setting up of a new mechanism for local artists to apply for the Chinese National Arts Fund run by the Chinese government, which previously was only open to applications within mainland China.[26]

More directly impacting local art groups and businesses is the 2022 establishment of a new government bureau. As part of a government reshuffle, the Culture, Sports and Tourism Bureau took over a vast portfolio including the Leisure and Cultural Services Department (which runs many local museums and the city's public libraries) and the Hong Kong Arts Development Council.[27] The minister in charge, Kevin Yeung, is a career civil servant who was previously the Secretary for Education.[28] He and other officials in the new bureau have turned down interview requests for this book. However, there are plenty of public statements regarding the bureau's priorities, and it is expected to publish a ten-year blueprint for the city's arts and culture development.

One of the bureau's key roles is to use the arts to promote China's soft power internationally. As an international centre of cultural exchange, Hong Kong will 'extend the reach of Chinese culture and tell good stories of China to the world'.[29] The cultural sector is also seen to have great economic potential. For example, the bureau is tasked with administering a Mega Arts and Cultural Events Fund to help drive tourism and spending.[30] Recipients of the fund include Art Basel Hong Kong, which received HK$15 million out of the HK$1.1 billion fund in 2024, and the *Chubby Hearts Hong Kong* exhibition by British designer Anya Hindmarch, which received HK$7.8 million for putting up giant heart-shaped balloons around town.[31] It will continue the government's previously announced focus on boosting 'Art Tech' as well as promoting cultural integration within the new Greater Bay Area comprising Hong Kong, Macau and nine municipalities in Guangdong province on the mainland.

Art Business as Usual?

Culture Minister Kevin Yeung has repeatedly denied that the NSL has had an impact on arts development in the city, reassuring practitioners that there is still a lot of freedom and room for manoeuvre as long as they abide by local laws.[32] Despite the stubbornly slow post-pandemic economy in Hong Kong and China, the high-end art businesses already in Hong Kong are digging their heels in.[33] Back in 2019–21 there were Western galleries which said that their artists refused to show their art in Hong Kong after the police crackdown on protesters, and international practitioners were among the 1500 who signed a widely circulated petition expressing concerns about the NSL and the loss of freedom in the city.[34] Today it is more common to hear a version of what some would describe as 'whataboutism': what about the limitations on freedoms shown up in the West by the recent culture wars or the Gaza protests in the US?

Among those who are giving the Hong Kong government the benefit of the doubt is art dealer Marc Glimcher, CEO of Pace, the American mega-gallery which closed its Beijing space in 2019 and made Hong Kong the centre of its China operations:[35]

> The worst part in 2019 and 2020 was that the artists started telling me they were not interested in having a show in Hong Kong. That would be the death knell if it continued. They were so interested in showing in Seoul. Same for Japan. Getting that enthusiasm for showing in Hong Kong is the challenge. It has come back but it is definitely not as strong as before.[36]

Galleries have certainly expanded their regional footprint since the pandemic, and new art fairs such as Frieze Seoul, Tokyo Gendai and Art SG are competitors to Art Basel Hong Kong. And in 2024 Pace opened a new gallery in Tokyo's Thomas Heatherwick-designed Azabudai Hills development, partly because of a fresh wave of optimism about the country's economy but also because the country has always had great allure for artists.

But to say Hong Kong is done would be 'insane', Glimcher states: 'Hong Kong has had a bad couple of years but you can't replace it as a pan-Asian meeting spot. I can't run an Asian operation without Hong Kong.' He is excited by China's contemporary art scene and expects the country's art market, including Hong Kong's, to recover by 2027. The city, which remains a free port and a more open environment than mainland

China, is still where Chinese collectors 'make their opinions' about art, he believes. With many people seeing London's share of the art market decline after Brexit, and the Labour government's plan to scrap non-domiciled tax status, the bets are still on Hong Kong to become a close rival to New York as the world's most important art market, according to Patti Wong, former Chair in Asia at Sotheby's. She has bought at least two paintings by Gustav Klimt in the two years since she launched her own advisory business in 2023, and is one of the best-connected operators in the art industry, with clients such as Taiwanese collector Pierre Chen.[37]

But the global art market certainly began 2024 in a state of torpor, and in Hong Kong, where the market is highly correlated to the slowing Chinese economy, total sales from the Sotheby's, Christie's and Phillips's Spring marquee evening auctions dropped 40 per cent from the previous year.[38] More worryingly, some economists have warned of a downward structural deceleration of China's luxury market due to a number of factors – slower economy, slower rise in disposable income, a weak currency and the government's crackdown on ostentatious spending.[39] And in July 2024 Lévy Gorvy Dayan + Wei announced it was closing its physical branch in Hong Kong. In 2019 it had been one of the last major international art galleries to launch a new space in the city. Rebecca Wei, its partner based in Asia, put the closure down to a change in client behaviour. She told the *Financial Times* that, after the pandemic, her regional clients in their fifties no longer wanted to travel to Hong Kong and preferred to purchase art remotely. The gallery will still operate as a Hong Kong business, she added, just without a saleroom.[40]

Hong Kong's post-pandemic economic recovery remains patchy at the time of writing. But Western auction houses are making bullish bets on the city one after another. As mentioned earlier, Christie's was the first to announce in 2021 that it had outgrown the twice-yearly auction seasons at the Hong Kong Convention and Exhibition Centre and was switching to having year-round auctions. In September 2024, it inaugurated its lavish 50,000 square-foot new headquarters at The Henderson with major sales of Chinese works of art and an evening sale that included works by Vincent van Gogh and Claude Monet. In 2023, Phillips opened its new Asia headquarters outside M+ museum, becoming the first of the big three Western houses to hold auctions in its own venue. 'There is still a lot of potential in this market. When it comes to Hong Kong, it's really serving the greater China market. Three quarters of our transactional activity comes from Greater China, whether it's Hong Kong, Taiwan or the mainland', says Jonathan Crockett, Phillips's Chairman of Asia and Head of 20th Century and Contemporary Art.[41]

Sotheby's own 'Maison', a 24,000 square-foot space, opened in the summer of 2024 inside the upmarket Landmark shopping centre in Central. A large retail section that includes pieces priced as low as US$645 indicates a new strategy, though the house also signalled its confidence in the top end of the market by leading its inaugural auction at the Landmark with a painting by Mark Rothko. Two new art fairs have also been announced, so far. In 2024 Art021, a Shanghai-based operation that previously only ran fairs on the mainland, launched its first Hong Kong edition in the last week of August. Photofairs, which has had an annual fair in Shanghai since 2014, will be held next to the main satellite fair Art Central during Art Basel week in March 2025. It remains to be seen whether the new fairs can be sustained when government subsidies for 'mega events' run out, or whether, like Art Basel did in 2013, they signal a new phase of bullishness about Hong Kong's art market.

The fact that there are over 200 billionaires and over 86 million people living in the Greater Bay Area (GBA) – more than Germany and far more than the UK or France – presents an enticing catchment prospect for Hong Kong's art market, says Damian Chandler, a cultural and public relations consultant in Hong Kong who has advised regional private museums. 'However, the extent to which these uber-rich will invest in art is the chronic question', he adds.[42] Hong Kong will always appeal to the wealthy across various sectors given its solid business practices, transparent regulations, governance and de facto free port, he believes. Its museums can also seed a burgeoning art market and appreciation for art across the GBA, while acknowledging that 'there is strong competition across the region to pull those serious buyers and eyes'.

Adjusting to the New Hong Kong

Market prospects aside, artists and art professionals continue to adjust to Hong Kong's new political reality and national security laws. Henry Tang, Chairman of the West Kowloon Cultural District, says that M+ has shown how it is possible to defend its curatorial independence against attacks from populist politicians and nationalist bloggers calling for the removal of works deemed critical of the Chinese government, as mentioned in Chapter 4. While the most provocative pieces are no longer seen in public, he maintains that the museum has not compromised its values and that its permanent collection is intact. He urges all practitioners, institutions and businesses to stand behind any art unless the courts have declared it illegal. 'You saw us. We pushed back very strongly. We had very strong ground to stand up on. I said, everyone must abide by the law. That's Hong Kong', he says.[43]

Despite the Secretary for Security's 'soft resistance' warnings, Tang does not believe the government plans to extend official censorship beyond films:

I am not aware of any government wish to impose censorship on artwork and art displays in Hong Kong. I have not heard any rumour, and I don't think they will do that. If they are going to do that, are they going to start censoring books as well? Start censoring your book? Start censoring newspapers? Where will that end?

'In the past we have seen radicals at the other end', Tang states, meaning those who were anti-China and wanted to fight for Hong Kong independence. 'Now we see some radicals from the other end, who are strongly against Gay Games, for example', he adds, referring to the seven conservative, nationalist lawmakers who claimed that the 2023 international sports event was an attempt to subvert national security. Their argument? The Gay Games amounted to the sugar-coating of Western ideology in the name of promoting diversity and inclusivity.[44] Diversity is Hong Kong's main strength, Tang believes, as is its rule of law.

The Myth-makers

The Gay Games did go ahead in November 2023, with the support of Regina Ip, a prominent government advisor and pro-Beijing lawmaker. Apart from a fringe group who link LGBTQ rights with a threat to national security, Hong Kong still has a sizeable and vocal conservative Christian community that is fiercely against same-sex marriage or civil unions, which are not offered in the city. But compared with mainland China – some would say, certain states in the US as well – Hong Kong is still far more liberal in general, with new laws passed in recent years that have improved LGBTQ rights.

A sign of this liberal atmosphere was the Queer art exhibition *Myth Makers – Spectrosynthesis III*,[45] which marked Hong Kong's reopening in December 2022. This large-scale show was held at Tai Kwun and supported by Sunpride Foundation, home to a collection of LGBTQ art owned by Hong Kong businessman Patrick Sun. It featured works by over sixty artists from Asia and its diasporas, curated along the idea of 'Queer mythologies' – an apt theme in a city that also believes in creating its own myths and identity. At the opening party, attended by hundreds of guests and featuring an electric performance by local art duo Virtual Village, the comment most heard was: 'At least Hong Kong still allows this'.

New artist collectives and exhibitions have also appeared recently to bring visibility and understanding to the many different artist communities in Hong Kong, including practitioners who have physical disabilities and, also, art by marginalised communities such as the foreign domestic workers from the Philippines and Indonesia who make up nearly 5 per cent of the total population.

Moving On

Some artists and curators familiar with the more restrictive environments on the mainland and elsewhere are urging their Hong Kong colleagues to keep calm and carry on. Beijing-based artist Wang Tuo says he was glad to have been able to premiere his art film about censorship, called

The Second Interrogation, during Art Basel Hong Kong in March 2023. He feels it was a test of Hong Kong's limits and it proved that the city is still much freer than mainland China.[46]

Billy Tang, the British-Vietnamese curator who worked in Beijing and Shanghai for ten years before becoming the Executive Director of Para Site in 2022, sees such a comparison as reductive however. 'It is not a competition', he says, pointing out that a lot of art that is challenging and provocative gets shown on the mainland, too.[47] Hong Kong's main difference from the mainland is the maturity and diversity of the contemporary art ecosystem, where nonprofits such as Para Site and the Asia Art Archive have played specific and consistent roles. He is also a firm believer that tough times breed great art: 'Globally, it is very complicated right now. Through adversity or difficult questions, the best of art can arise and comes to the surface.'

Pi Li, the Beijing-born Head of Art at Tai Kwun, who has lived in Hong Kong since 2012, continues to voice confidence in the city's art scene. The point he frequently makes is that the city remains far more open than mainland China and the growing number of world-class art institutions means that Hong Kong, to him, is the only place where international dialogue about Chinese art can happen. That role for Hong Kong has become more important when mainland China is, as it is today, more opaque to the rest of the world, he said during a panel discussion in September 2024.[48]

Curators have noted that there was an effective ban on showing Hong Kong art on the mainland immediately after the 2019 protest, as the Chinese authorities feared the spreading of dissent. So it was especially encouraging to see artists such as Natalie Lo Lai-lai, a Hong Kong artist whose practice has to do with environmentalism and local identity, having a solo show across the border in Shenzhen in December 2023, with support from the Hong Kong Arts Development Council. The artist-cum-farmer has been making contemplative films and installations that challenge anthropocentrism while also creating an alternative Hong Kong narrative from the perspective of its marginalised and underappreciated rural values.

Lo's practice is an example of how, in the face of massive government projects to develop the still-green northern New Territories in order to promote economic integration with China, a socially engaged artist has continued to create critical, urgent and relevant works. Her exhibition, evocatively titled *As Shards of Dawn Shot Through the Dark*, found a receptive audience in Shenzhen, where the pace of development has been among the most dramatic in China. As the Hong Kong-based curator Chris Wan says, there may be mutual suspicion between Hong Kong and mainland China, but art really can transcend ideological boundaries.[49]

Having a positive mind-set matters, says Tozer Pak Sheung-chuen, a well-established conceptual artist in Hong Kong who represented the city in the 2009 Venice Biennale and whose works are collected by M+, Tate in London and other international museums. Since 2003 he has been making works associated with Hong Kong's political changes. 'I really struggled for the last three years. I used to publish my work through a newspaper. But after 2020, everything changed. I know that works directly touching on politics will no longer be published easily', he says.[50] Today, he teaches in a Taiwan university for part of the year, while in Hong Kong he has co-founded a collective called Hass Lab that advocates art thinking as a new way of seeing the world.

Gone but Not Forgotten

As mentioned in Chapter 3, many art practitioners have left Hong Kong for various reasons in recent years. Husband-and-wife duo C&G Artpartment, now based in Sheffield in the UK, have continued their socially engaged practice with initiatives such as *Harcourt Road* (2024). Named after a road that exists both in Hong Kong and in Sheffield, the project invited local people to share stories and objects while the artists shared their own memories of Hong Kong with their new neighbours.

Asymmetry Art Foundation, founded by former Hong Kong resident Yan Du, is a new non-profit in London dedicated to cross-cultural art research which has set up fellowships in the UK. A number of Hong Kong practitioners are among those who have benefited, and they have helped to spread knowledge about Hong Kong's art scene in the country. And my erstwhile colleague at the *South China Morning Post*, Vivienne Chow, continues to report on Hong Kong's art scene and its diaspora art community from her new base in London.

While the more politically active artists and art professionals may not feel that it is safe for them to return to Hong Kong, many practitioners who have left for other countries since 2019 have returned for visits or for longer projects. Amid an ongoing talent shortage across different sectors, there has been exciting new blood, too, such as well-established curators joining Para Site (Billy Tang) and M+ (Russell Storer) from overseas. Since the pandemic, the city has launched numerous 'talent schemes' that make it easier for outsiders to obtain work visas.

A bastion of intermedia art in Asia since the 1990s, Hong Kong also offers plenty of opportunity for artists to experiment in an age when different media and new technology increasingly converge. In 1998 the City University of Hong Kong established Asia's first tertiary-level school of creative media and, ten years later, Melbourne-born new-media pioneer Jeffrey Shaw took over as Dean and broadened its focus from lens-based art to new technology. It continues to be one of the most cosmopolitan and forward-thinking art schools in the region.

Shaw is now at Hong Kong Baptist University's Academy of Visual Arts, where he has a well-funded laboratory for developing 'next-generation art technologies'. Meanwhile, important work is being done on the ethics of AI and the arts at a number of institutions. A sizeable community of locally and overseas-trained mixed-media artists such as Orlean Lai, Kingsley Ng and the artist known as GayBird are able to tap into ample government funding for 'arts tech' for interesting projects. And there is also support for large-scale technological experimentation by artists from the inimitable Agnes Lin, whose Osage Gallery and non-profit foundation have consistently presented quality exhibitions since 2004.

It is important to note, however, that there have been com-plaints about directing too much resource to 'arts tech' ever since the government set aside HK$100 million (US$12.8 million) to its development in 2020.[51] Hong Kong is also affected by what many describe as a US-led effort to restrict China's access to advanced AI technology. For example, ChatGPT's creator OpenAI blocks access from mainland China and Hong Kong.[52]

Meanwhile, the city's artistic community has become more tight-knit and collaborative because of recent challenges, says Eunice Tsang, founder of Current Plans. After she lost her original space in Sham Shui Po due to gentrification and a hike in rent, art patron Mimi Brown offered her the temporary use of a large space in Wong Chuk Hang where Brown used to run Spring Workshop, a pioneer of cross-disciplinary collaborations from 2011 to 2018. Tsang told me: 'I hope to revive the conviviality of Spring Workshop. Hong Kong has its challenges but there are still plenty of people who are starting new projects and trying new ways of doing things.'[53]

At the other end of the scale, artist South Ho's space 100-ft. PARK (named after its small size – 100 square feet), founded in 2012, was relaunched in 2022 as New Park, with new partners Michelle Wong Wun-ting, an art historian and curator, and Billy H.C. Kwok, a photographer and journalist. In a seminar on the importance of Hong Kong's independent art spaces, Wong said that the still-intimate space (though a bit bigger at 400 square feet) allows for experimentation and conversations to be had freely outside of large institutions lumbered with bureaucracy, fulfilling an important function of bringing the art community together after the 2014 and 2019 protests and social ruptures.[54]

Arthur de Villepin, who opened his family-owned gallery in Hong Kong's central business district right in the middle of the 2019 protests, thinks that the city needs a deeper rethink about what it needs, rather than just carrying on building more of the same. Villepin says he is committed to staying: 'If Hong Kong keeps having more, more, more, it will lose meaning. We need a real vision that isn't just to sell more, or build more art storage facilities. We need to make Hong Kong a place that people want to visit. Then the collectors will follow.'[55]

It is encouraging to see new businesses arriving that can help the art market in Hong Kong move up the value chain. For example, HSBC has begun offering art-secured lending options to their private banking clients, and a number of major US banks are also offering such services. In May 2024 Italy's Generali Group made Hong Kong the Asia launch pad for its art insurance solutions. And, in the summer of 2024, Hong Kong art collector Lewis Cheng soft-launched a new art logistics company borne out of his frustration with existing options. The company, Eythos, is building warehouses in Hong Kong and in Seoul that offer specialist storage facilities for different kinds of artworks as well as end-to-end carbon accounting for each work.

Despite Hong Kong's many challenges and the threat of funding drying up, the pile-driving and the drilling continue in the West Kowloon Cultural District. Gesturing to the hive of activity taking place inside and around M+, Suhanya Raffel says she can't help feeling that Hong Kong remains one of the most exciting places in the world:

> We are working together with the international global museum community and the impact of Covid on our institutions has been profound. All of us have had to respond to that situation and change and relook at our business plans. In that respect, I feel that Asia is far more stable than parts of North America and the UK. So, you know, comparatively, we are in a better place primarily because this part of the world is still growing economically.
>
> As with any situation, where there's risk, there's opportunity. And I've seen Hong Kong artists embrace that opportunity. There is a very serious shift in the political and social environment of the city. But then, you know, I speak to so many colleagues who say, with Hong Kong, you can never write it off. I think the city's energy and grit is a spirit that I really respond to and respect. I feel that a city like Hong Kong has a lot to offer the world and we will continue to find ways of retrieving what that means.[56]

Notes

The abbreviation *SCMP* stands for *South China Morning Post* throughout the notes.

Introduction: What is Hong Kong?

1   Christopher Johnson, 'What Deng Taught Xi Jinping: Pragmatism Trumps Ideology', *East Asia Forum*, 28 September 2013, https://eastasiaforum. org/2013/09/28/what-deng-taught-xi-jinping-pragmatism-trumps-ideology/.

2   John M. Carroll, *A Concise History of Hong Kong*, Hong Kong University Press, Hong Kong, 2007, pp 140–66.

3   Fang Xue, 'Chan: Innovation, Financial Industries Give GBA Edge over Rivals', *China Daily*, 21 May 2024, https://www.chinadailyhk.com/hk/ article/583732.

4   Zhou Mo, 'GBA to Play Vital Role in Promoting Chinese Culture and Fostering Unity', *China Daily*, 9 June 2023, https://www.chinadailyhk.com/ hk/article/335177.

5   Greater Bay Area official website, Hong Kong Constitutional and Mainland Affairs Bureau, https://www.bayarea.gov.hk/gbais/en/development/cultural-sports-and-tourism-co-operation/.

6   William Xu, 'HK to Boost Patriotic Education, Chinese Culture Appreciation', *China Daily*, 25 October 2023, https://www.chinadailyhk.com/ hk/article/358002.

1: Art in Hong Kong

1   'How Hong Kong Became One of the Most Unequal Places in the World',
    Stanford University Center on China's Economy and Institutions, 1 March
    2024, https://sccei.fsi.stanford.edu/china-briefs/how-hong-kong-became-
    one-most-unequal-places-world.

2   This and subsequent quotes, Jaffa Lam, conversation with the author, January
    2024.

3   Tao Wang, 'Lui Shou-kwan's Zen Painting and American Abstraction', Art
    Institute of Chicago, 5 July 2023, https://www.artic.edu/articles/1067/lui-shou-
    kwan-s-zen-painting-and-american-abstraction.

4   Edited transcript of John Chan Koon-chung's talk at Hong Kong Baptist
    University (in Chinese), BBC, 29 October 2019, https://www.bbc.com/
    zhongwen/simp/chinese-news-50217104.

5   'Tourists Will See New-look HK Is No Cultural Desert', *RTHK*, 24 January
    2023, https://news.rthk.hk/rthk/en/component/k2/1685093-20230124.htm.

6   May Holdsworth and Christopher Munn, *Dictionary of Hong Kong Biography*,
    Hong Kong University Press, Hong Kong, 2012, pp 242–3.

7   Nigel Cameron, 'Hong Kong: The Development of Modern Art', *Hong
    Kong Art Review*, AICA – The International Association of Art Critics,
    1999, p.60.

8   Lawrence C.S. Tam, 'Introduction', in *Hong Kong Art 1970–80*, The Hong
    Kong Museum of Art, Hong Kong, 1981, pp 6–12.

9   At the same time, it is worth bearing in mind that historians have pointed
    out that the rules of the Cold War were often suspended in Hong Kong in
    the decades after the Second World War, with confrontations tempered by
    pragmatism and flexibility. See, for example, Priscilla Roberts, 'Cold War
    Hong Kong: Juggling Opposing Forces and Identities', *Hong Kong in the Cold
    War*, Hong Kong University Press, Hong Kong, 2016, pp 26–59.

10 David Clarke, *Art & Place*, Hong Kong University Press, Hong Kong, 1996,
    pp 24–5.

11 Oscar Ho Hing-kay, 'Inventing History', *Hong Kong Art Review*, AICA – The
    International Association of Art Critics, 1999, p.48.

12 Oscar Ho Hing-kay, 'Lo Ting and Hong Kong Cultural Identity: Part One',
    Asia Art Archive, 24 September 2021, https://aaa.org.hk/en/like-a-fever/like-
    a-fever/lo-ting-and-hong-kong-cultural-identity-part-one.

13 Clarke, *Art & Place*, p.76.

14 Ackbar Abbas, 'The New Hong Kong Cinema and the "Déjà Disparu"', *Discourse*, vol.16, no.3, 1994, p.67.

15 See, for example, Joan Kee, 'Art, Hong Kong, and Hybridity: A Task of Reconsideration', *Yishu: Journal of Contemporary Chinese Art*, vol.2, no.2, June 2003, p.94.

16 Ho Hing-kay, 'Inventing History', p.48.

17 Frank Vigneron, *I Like Hong Kong: Art and Deterritorialization*, The Chinese University Press, Hong Kong, 2010, pp 133–72.

18 Vivian Poon, 'The Lasting Impact of Hong Kong's New Ink Movement', *Artbasel*, 20 February 2024, https://www.artbasel.com/stories/hong-kong-new-ink-movement.

19 Bernard Hung-kay Luk, 'Chinese Culture in the Hong Kong Curriculum: Heritage and Colonialism', *Comparative Education Review*, vol.35, no.4, November 1991, pp 667–8.

20 The Hong Kong Art Biennial Exhibition, which later became the Hong Kong Contemporary Art Biennial Awards, was hosted by the Hong Kong Museum of Art from 1975 to 2012 as a purely local affair, unlike the large-scale, international biennials and triennials in other parts of Asia.

21 David Clarke, *Hong Kong Art: Culture and Decolonization*, Hong Kong University Press, Hong Kong, 2001, pp 7–69; Vennes Cheng, 'The Misrepresentation of Hong Kongness: The Revamped Hong Kong Museum of Art', *Museum Worlds*, vol.8, no.1, 2020, pp 149–67.

22 Enid Tsui, 'Levitation and Levity in 2022 Venice Biennale's Hong Kong Pavilion, with Angela Su's Video Art and Hair Embroideries', *SCMP*, 25 April 2022, https://www.scmp.com/lifestyle/arts-culture/article/3175407/levitation-and-levity-2022-venice-biennales-hong-kong.

23 Anthony Yung, 'Opaque, Impenetrably Concealed Secrecy – A Reading Guide to Ellen Pau and "Inauspicious Symbol"', *Kiang Malingue*, 7 November 2023, https://kiangmalingue.com/wordpress/wp-content/uploads/2023/11/Eng_Ellen-Pau_article_20231107.pdf.

24 Winnie Wong, 'On Smallness in Hong Kong Art', *M+ Stories*, undated, https://www.mplus.org.hk/en/magazine/on-smallness-in-hong-kong-art/.

25 Kacey Wong, Justin Wong and artist duo C&G Artpartment form part of a growing population of diaspora Hong Kong artists, which will be discussed in Chapter 5.

26 The colonial administrations from the 1960s to the 1980s are often venerated by neo-liberals as the architects of Hong Kong's post-war economic

growth. Critics blame their legacy of laissez-faire and minimal government interference for the deep-seated inequality and structural weaknesses in the city that remain today. See, for example, Tang Hei-wai, 'The 50-year Impact of Positive Non-interventionism on Hong Kong', Asia Global Institute, 14 April 2021, https://www.asiaglobalinstitute.hku.hk/storage/app/media/Op-eds/The%2050-year%20Impact%20of%20Positive%20Non-interventionism%20on%20Hong%20Kong.pdf.

27   Anthony Leung Po-shan, *I Love Art Basel,* dirty press, Hong Kong, 2018.

28   Asia Art Archive researcher Anthony Yung, conversation with the author, 9 January 2024.

29   Clarke, *Hong Kong Art*, p.166.

30   Oliver Giles, 'Why Was Jaffa Lam Going to Burn All Her Art?', *Zolima City Mag*, 21 March 2023, https://zolimacitymag.com/why-was-jaffa-lam-going-to-burn-all-her-art/.

2: 'Cultural Desert' No More

1   Vicki Ooi, 'The Best Cultural Policy Is No Cultural Policy: Cultural Policy in Hong Kong', *The European Journal of Cultural Policy*, vol.1, no.2, 1995, pp 273–87.

2   See, for example, Gary Ka-wai Cheung, *Hong Kong's Watershed: The 1967 Riots*, Hong Kong University Press, Hong Kong, 2009.

3   Gary Cheung, 'The Secret Handover', *SCMP*, 20 November 2006, https://www.scmp.com/article/572242/secret-handover.

4   'Exhibition on History of the Urban Council Opens Today', Hong Kong government press release, 28 December 1999, https://www.info.gov.hk/gia/general/199912/28/1228209.htm.

5   Tsang Kai-won, 'Museums in Late Colonial Hong Kong', MPhil thesis, University of Hong Kong, 2020, pp 99–101, https://hub.hku.hk/handle/10722/283111.

6   For a list of major donors to the Hong Kong Museum of Art, see https://hk.art.museum/en/web/ma/collections/major-donors.html.

7   'History of the Hong Kong Arts Centre', https://hkac.org.hk/about_history/.

8   'The Property Market and the Macro-economy', *Hong Kong Monetary Authority Quarterly Bulletin*, May 2001, https://www.hkma.gov.hk/media/eng/publication-and-research/quarterly-bulletin/qb200105/fa02.pdf.

9   Christopher DeWolf, 'At Site of Hong Kong's First Artists' Village, Art Has

Come Full Circle', *SCMP*, 1 March 2020, https://www.scmp.com/lifestyle/travel-leisure/article/3048327/site-hong-kongs-first-artists-village-art-has-come-full.

10 John Batten, 'The Origins of Hong Kong's Independent Art Spaces', *International Association of Art Critics Hong Kong*, 23 April 2008, http://www.aicahk.org/eng/spacedetail.asp?catid=39.

11 Lam Tung-pang, 'From Fo Tan to Fotanian', 2011, artist's website, http://www.lamtungpang.com/writings/files/10fd92cbd8a8a4bc83ed5c5f415d4065-0.html.

12 *Private to Public: The History of Chinese Art Collecting in Hong Kong*, Hong Kong Palace Museum, 2 July–31 December 2022, wall texts available from https://virtualmuseum.hkpm.org.hk/en-past-exhibitions/private-to-public-the-history-of-chinese-art-collecting-in-hong-kong.

13 Nicolas Chow, interview with the author, June 2023.

14 Mamie Howe, née Dunn, was the elder sister of Lydia, who by the 1970s had become a powerful business and political figure in colonial Hong Kong. Lydia Dunn was elevated to the peerage by Queen Elizabeth II in 1990 and she moved to the UK in 1996 after playing a major role in determining Hong Kong's future after its 1997 return to China.

15 'A Pioneer in Auction Business', Mamie Howe obituary, *SCMP*, 22 February 1987.

16 Kejia Wu, *A Modern History of China's Art Market*, Routledge, Abingdon & New York, 2023, pp 29–57.

17 Nicolas Chow, interview with the author, June 2023.

18 Joyce Hor-chung Lau, 'Frame of Reference', *SCMP*, 18 April 2004, https://www.scmp.com/article/452559/frame-reference.

19 Elizabeth Yuen, 'Painting's Owner "Un-Executed"', *CNN*, 12 October 2007, https://edition.cnn.com/2007/WORLD/asiapcf/10/12/china.artist/.

20 Farhad Taghizadeh-Hesary, Naoyuki Yoshino and Alvin Chiu, 'Internal and External Determinants of Housing Price Booms in Hong Kong, China', *ADBI Working Paper Series*, Asian Development Bank Institute, Tokyo, 2019.

21 Barbara Pollack, 'The Chinese Art Explosion', *Artnews*, 1 September 2008, https://www.artnews.com/art-news/news/the-chinese-art-explosion-206/.

22 'China Antiques & Artworks Auction Market Statistical Annual Report', *China Association of Auctioneers*, November 2023, https://amma.artron.net/reportDetail.php?id=116.

23 'The Art Market in 2023', *Artprice*, https://www.artprice.com/artprice-reports/the-art-market-in-2023/our-global-ranking-of-auction-houses.

24 Guo Tong, interview with the author, 18 July 2023.

25 Melanie Gerlis, *The Art Fair Story: A Rollercoaster Ride*, Hot Topics in the Art World, Lund Humphries, London, 2021, p.58.

26 Sarah Cascone, 'Art Basel Completes Hong Kong Art Fair Buy-Out', *Artnet*, 28 October 2014, https://news.artnet.com/market/art-basel-completes-hong-kong-art-fair-buy-out-144479.

27 Gerlis, *The Art Fair Story*, pp 59–60.

28 Amy Qin, 'With Modigliani Purchase, Chinese Billionaire Dreams of Bigger Canvas', *New York Times*, 17 November 2015, https://www.nytimes.com/2015/11/18/arts/international/with-modigliani-purchase-chinese-billionaire-liu-yiqian-dreams-of-bigger-canvas.html.

29 Sarah Cascone, 'Chinese Billionaire Liu Yiqian Is the Buyer for the Record-Breaking $170-Million Modigliani Nude', *Artnet*, 10 November 2015, https://news.artnet.com/market/liu-yiqian-modigliani-170-million-360029.

30 'Central Still the World's Most Expensive Office Market, Despite Rental Gap with Mainland Chinese Cities Narrowing', *JLL*, https://www.jll.com.mo/en/newsroom/premium-office-rent-tracker.

31 Anny Shaw, 'Gallerist Ben Brown on Hong Kong's Art Scene', *Financial Times*, 22 March 2019, https://www.ft.com/content/51f4e166-496f-11e9-bde6-79eaea5acb64.

32 Pace's first Hong Kong gallery was set up in 2014 in a smaller space in Entertainment Building.

33 Magnus Renfrew, *Uncharted Territory: Culture and Commerce in Hong Kong's Art World*, Penguin, London, 2017, pp 16–17.

3: Art in a Time of Crisis

1 Andrew Mullen, 'US-China Trade War Timeline', *SCMP*, 29 August 2021, https://www.scmp.com/economy/china-economy/article/3146489/us-china-trade-war-timeline-key-dates-and-events-july-2018.

2 'Chinese State Media Defend Hong Kong Visa Refusal for FT Journalist', *Reuters*, 8 October 2018.

3 Tony Cheung, 'What Is Behind Hong Kong's Anti-Extradition Protests?', *SCMP*, 13 June 2019, https://www.scmp.com/news/hong-kong/politics/article/3014261/what-behind-hong-kongs-anti-extradition-protests.

4 'Hong Kong National Security Law: What Is It and Is It Worrying?', *BBC News*, 28 June 2022, https://www.bbc.com/news/world-asia-china-52765838.

5   Tom Grundy, 'Hong Kong's Lady Liberty Statue Vandalised after Being Installed atop Lion Rock', *hongkongfp*, 14 October 2019, https://hongkongfp.com/2019/10/14/hong-kongs-lady-liberty-statue-vandalised-installed-atop-lion-rock/.

6   Alice Woodhouse and Nicolle Liu, 'Hong Kong Protesters Go into Creative Overdrive', *Financial Times*, 16 October 2019, https://www.ft.com/content/526e2d46-ee97-11e9-bfa4-b25f11f42901.

7   Keith Richburg, 'Chinese Artist Ai Weiwei Arrested in Ongoing Government Crackdown', *Washington Post*, 3 April 2011, https://www.washingtonpost.com/world/chinese-artist-ai-wei-wei-arrested-in-latest-government-crackdown/2011/04/03/AFHB5PVC_story.html; Bernice Chan, 'My Life: Kacey Wong Kwok-Choi', *SCMP*, 29 November 2014, https://www.scmp.com/magazines/post-magazine/article/1649865/my-life-kacey-wong-kwok-choi.

8   En Liang Khong, 'Hong Kong and the Art of Dissent', *Financial Times*, 6 December 2019, https://www.ft.com/content/438210e8-16bc-11ea-8d73-6303645ac406.

9   'The Five Commandments', *Kaceywong.com*, https://www.kaceywong.com/the-five-commandments.

10   Aaina Bhargava, 'Artists' Reflections on Destructive Power of Nature Take on New Meaning After Hong Kong's Summer of Protest', *SCMP*, 15 September 2019, https://www.scmp.com/lifestyle/arts-culture/article/3027156/artists-reflections-destructive-power-nature-take-new.

11   Chow Chun-fai, interview with the author, 2020.

12   Aaina Bhargava, 'Hong Kong Protest Art: "Dystopia" of Street Violence Captured in Paintings Taut with Emotion', *SCMP*, 14 March 2020, https://www.scmp.com/lifestyle/arts-culture/article/3075028/hong-kong-protest-art-dystopia-street-violence-captured.

13   Enid Tsui, 'Hong Kong Pavilion at Venice Biennale Closes Amid Extradition Bill Protests', *SCMP*, 11 June 2019, https://www.scmp.com/lifestyle/arts-culture/article/3014068/art-galleries-close-hong-kong-extradition-bill-protest-and.

14   Enid Tsui, 'Is This the End of Physical Art Galleries in Hong Kong?', *SCMP*, 3 March 2020, https://www.scmp.com/magazines/post-magazine/arts-music/article/3052448/end-physical-art-galleries-hong-kong-not-only.

15   Tessa Solomon, 'Lévy Gorvy Dayan to Close Hong Kong Space', *Artnews*, 7 July 2024, https://www.artnews.com/art-news/news/levy-gorvy-dayan-closes-

hong-kong-branch-1234711594/.

16 Noah Horowitz, interview with the author, 17 January 2024.

17 Art Basel press release, 21 November 2023, https://www.artbasel.com/stories/
    art-basel-hong-kong-returns-to-full-scale-for-its-2024-edition?lang=en.

18 Tim Schneider, 'Hong Kong's Art Auctions Declined in the First Major Slate
    of Sales Since Political Protests Engulfed the City', *Artnet*, 16 December 2019,
    https://news.artnet.com/market/hong-kong-protests-fall-sales-1734654.

19 Aaina Bhargava, 'Art Basel: Hong Kong Galleries Back Organiser Amid Calls
    to Cancel Fair Over Protests, Coronavirus Emergency', *SCMP*, 1 February
    2020, https://www.scmp.com/lifestyle/arts-culture/article/3048469/art-basel-
    hong-kong-galleries-back-organiser-amid-calls.

20 Natalie Wong and Lilian Cheng, 'Coronavirus: Hong Kong Urged to
    Maintain "Dynamic Zero-Covid" Policy, with Beijing Officials and State
    Media Warning Shift Will Mean Disaster for City', *SCMP*, 8 February 2022,
    https://www.scmp.com/news/hong-kong/health-environment/article/3166165/
    coronavirus-hong-kong-urged-maintain-dynamic-zero.

21 Laura Westbrook, 'Hong Kong Mother "Crying, Begging" After Hospital
    Separates Her From 11-Month-Old Baby Who Has Covid-19', *SCMP*, 22
    February 2022, https://www.scmp.com/news/hong-kong/health-environment/
    article/3167974/hong-kong-mother-crying-begging-after-hospital.

22 Lilian Cheng and Elizabeth Cheung, 'Hong Kong Now Has the World's
    Highest Covid-19 Death Rate', *SCMP*, 5 March 2022, https://www.scmp.
    com/news/hong-kong/health-environment/article/3169331/hong-kong-now-
    has-worlds-highest-covid-19-death.

23 Pak Yiu, 'Hong Kong Economy Shrinks 3.5% in 2022 on Covid Blues',
    Nikkei Asia, 1 February 2023, https://asia.nikkei.com/Economy/Hong-Kong-
    economy-shrinks-3.5-in-2022-on-COVID-blues.

24 Sheng Zhi Zhao, Janet Yuen Ha Wong, Tzu Tsun Luk, Abraham Ka
    Chung Wai, Tai Hing Lam, Man Ping Wang, 'Mental Health Crisis under
    COVID-19 Pandemic in Hong Kong, China', *International Journal of
    Infectious Diseases*, vol.100, 2020, pp 431–3.

25 ART Power HK, https://www.artpowerhk.com/.

26 Enid Tsui, 'Three Constrasting Art Exhibitions Grapple with the Big Issues
    Facing Hong Kong Today', *SCMP*, 20 March 2021, https://www.scmp.com/
    lifestyle/arts-culture/article/3126099/three-contrasting-art-exhibitions-
    grapple-big-issues-facing.

27 Enid Tsui, 'Christie's Hong Kong Spring Auctions Set Records for Art,

Wine and Watch Sales, with Sean Connery's Picasso Reaching US$22 Million', *SCMP*, 31 May 2022, https://www.scmp.com/lifestyle/arts-culture/article/3179816/christies-hong-kong-spring-auctions-set-records-art-wine-and.

28 Data supplied by ArtTactic, Poly Auction Hong Kong and China Guardian Hong Kong.

29 Guo Tong, interview with the author, 18 July 2023.

30 Angelica Villa, 'Sotheby's Added as Defendant in Investors' Lawsuit Over Marketing of Bored Ape Yacht Club NFTs', *Artnews*, 14 August 2023, https://www.artnews.com/art-news/news/sothebys-added-defendant-investors-lawsuit-bored-ape-yacht-club-nfts-1234677041/.

31 Guillaume Cerutti, interview with the author, 26 May 2023.

32 Karen K. Ho, 'ART SG Cofounder Magnus Renfrew Discusses Singapore's New Fair', *Artnews*, 10 January 2023, https://www.artnews.com/art-news/news/magnus-renfrew-art-sg-launch-interview-1234652999/.

33 Y-Jean Mun-Delsalle, 'Art SG, Southeast Asia's Largest Ever Art Fair, Launches Successfully in Singapore', *Forbes*, 13 January 2023, https://www.forbes.com/sites/yjeanmundelsalle/2023/01/13/art-sg-southeast-asias-largest-ever-art-fair-launches-successfully-in-singapore/.

34 Kimberly Lim and Su-lin Tan, 'Hong Kong's Talent Exodus to Singapore: Can It Be Reversed and Is "a New Wave of Expats" Inbound?', *SCMP*, 4 February 2023, https://www.scmp.com/week-asia/people/article/3209048/hong-kongs-talent-exodus-singapore-can-it-be-reversed-and-new-wave-expats-inbound.

35 'CE Statement on NPC's Deliberation on Improving HKSAR Electoral System to Implement "Patriots Administering Hong Kong"', Hong Kong government press release, 5 March 2021, https://www.info.gov.hk/gia/general/202103/05/P2021030500393.htm.

36 William Yiu, '150,400 Hongkongers Have Moved to UK Using BN(O) Pathway', *SCMP*, 22 August 2024, https://www.scmp.com/news/hong-kong/education/article/3253056/hard-replace-hongkongers-their-prime-biggest-group-lured-britains-bespoke-bno-migrant-scheme.

4: M+: Hong Kong's Global Museum

1 Amy Nip, 'West Kowloon Cultural District Should Be about Arts, Not Money, Experts Say', *SCMP*, 21 February 2014, https://www.scmp.com/news/

hong-kong/article/1432869/west-kowloon-cultural-district-should-be-about-arts-not-money-experts.

2   Vivienne Chow, 'A Series of Unfortunate Events: The Past and Present of West Kowloon Cultural District', *Cultural Vision*, May 2013, https://www.viviennechow.com/p/a-series-of-unfortunate-events-past-and.html.

3   'Pompidou, Guggenheim Join Forces', *SCMP*, 29 October 2005, https://www.scmp.com/article/522626/pompidou-guggenheim-join-forces.

4   'WKCD Museums Advisory Group Makes Innovative Recommendations', Hong Kong government press release, 23 November 2006, https://www.info.gov.hk/gia/general/200611/23/P200611230197.htm.

5   Holland Cotter, 'MoMA Reboots with "Modernism Plus"', *New York Times*, 10 October 2019, https://www.nytimes.com/2019/10/10/arts/design/moma-rehang-review-art.html.

6   Enid Tsui, 'All Eyes on M+, and Hong Kong, as Chinese Contemporary Art Exhibition Set to Open', *SCMP*, 20 February 2016, https://www.scmp.com/magazines/post-magazine/arts-entertainment/article/1913887/all-eyes-m--and-hong-kong-chinese.

7   Enid Tsui, 'Will the Art that Collector Uli Sigg Donated to Hong Kong Museum M+ Finally Be Judged on its Merits?', *SCMP*, 16 November 2021, https://www.scmp.com/magazines/post-magazine/long-reads/article/3133448/will-art-collector-uli-sigg-donated-hong-kong.

8   Uli Sigg, 'A Foreword to Viewing the M+ Sigg Collection', *Right is Wrong: Four Decades of Chinese Art from the M+ Sigg Collection*, Bildmuseet, Umeå, 2014, https://webmedia.mplus.org.hk/documents/Uli_Sigg_Foreword_to_Viewing_the_Mplus_Sigg_collection.pdf.

9   'Cheung Kong Graduate School of Business Professor Releases – the 2023 Annual MM Chinese Art Indices', Cheung Kong Graduate School of Business, 12 January 2024, https://english.ckgsb.edu.cn/knowledge/article/cheung-kong-graduate-school-of-business-professor-releases-the-2023-annual-mm-chinese-art-indices.

10 Enid Tsui, 'Lars Nittve: Why I'm Quitting Hong Kong Arts Hub Role', *SCMP*, 28 October 2015, https://www.scmp.com/lifestyle/arts-entertainment/article/1873107/lars-nittve-why-im-quitting-hong-kong-arts-hub-role.

11 'About the Collection', M+, https://www.mplus.org.hk/en/about-the-collection/.

12 Enid Tsui, 'M+ Opens At Last, a Museum of Contemporary Art and Design for the World, Amid a Culture War in Hong Kong, where Some Wonder if It

Belongs', *SCMP*, 12 November 2021, https://www.scmp.com/magazines/post-magazine/long-reads/article/3155751/m-opens-last-museum-contemporary-art-and-design.

13 Enid Tsui, 'Head of Hong Kong's M+ Museum Unfazed at Handling Political "Hot Potato" that is the West Kowloon Project', *SCMP*, 1 March 2017, https://www.scmp.com/culture/arts-entertainment/article/2074777/head-hong-kongs-future-m-museum-unfazed-handling-hot.

14 Suhanya Raffel, interview with the author, 9 June 2023.

15 Jaspar Lau, 'About the Controversy Caused by the HKADC and M+ over the Arrangement of the 2013 Venice Biennale Hong Kong Pavilion', *International Association of Art Critics Hong Kong*, 13 October 2012, http://www.aicahk.org/eng/issuesdetail.asp?id=321&pg=1.

16 Anqi Li, 'Bilbao Effect 2.0: The Making of M+', *Journal of Contemporary Chinese Art*, vol.11, no.1, April 2024, pp 13–30.

17 Lee Chesire, 'Hong Kong's M+ Museum Is among the 20 Most Visited Globally', *The Art Newspaper*, 28 March 2024, https://www.theartnewspaper.com/2024/03/28/hong-kongs-m+-museum-is-among-the-20-most-visited-globally.

18 Enid Tsui, 'New Hong Kong Museum Will Uphold Artistic Freedom, Director Says', *SCMP*, 12 March 2021, https://www.scmp.com/lifestyle/arts-culture/article/3125251/new-hong-kong-museum-will-uphold-artistic-freedom-director.

19 Amy Qin, 'Keeping Hong Kong Protest Art Alive Means Not Mothballing It', *New York Times*, 13 May 2016, https://www.nytimes.com/2016/05/14/arts/international/in-hong-kong-preserving-mementos-of-a-protest-movement.html.

20 Private conversation with the author.

21 Enid Tsui, 'Hong Kong Leader Vows to Protect Freedom of Expression after pro-Beijing Lawmaker Asks if New Museum Will Threaten National Security', *SCMP*, 17 March 2021, https://www.scmp.com/news/hong-kong/politics/article/3125854/hong-kong-leader-vows-protect-freedom-expression-pro.

22 Caroline Goldstein, 'An Artist Who Defended Ai Weiwei Has Resigned from Hong Kong's Arts Council, Citing "Personal Safety"', *Artnet*, 10 August 2021, https://news.artnet.com/art-world/hong-kong-arts-council-members-resign-1997079.

23 H.G. Masters, 'M+ Removes Controversial Paintings about Chinese History', *Art Asia Pacific*, 26 April 2022, https://artasiapacific.com/news/m-removes-controversial-paintings-about-chinese-history.

24 Tsui, 'Head of Hong Kong's M+ Museum Unfazed at Handling Political "Hot Potato"'.

25 Suhanya Raffel, interview with the author, 9 June 2023.

26 'M Plus Collections Limited', *West HK*, https://www.westkowloon.hk/en/m-plus-collections-limited.

27 Isabella Tam, interview with the author, March 2024.

28 Private conversation with the author, November 2021.

29 Yeewan Koon, 'Where Are We Now? M+ and the Uncertain Future of Hong Kong', *October*, vol.180, 2022, pp 150–64.

30 Suhanya Raffel, interview with the author, 9 June 2023.

31 Maria Balshaw, interview with the author, 20 March 2023.

32 Denise Tsang, 'Hong Kong West Kowloon Arts Hub Chief Says Funding Crisis Threatens Contracts for New Events', *SCMP*, 1 March 2024, https://www.scmp.com/news/hong-kong/hong-kong-economy/article/3253724/bounced-cheque-hong-kong-west-kowloon-arts-hub-chief-says-funding-crisis-threatens-contracts-new.

33 Sammy Heung, 'Hong Kong's West Kowloon Arts Hub to Sell Land Parcels in "a Few Years" Time, CEO Says', *SCMP*, 18 July 2024, https://www.scmp.com/news/hong-kong/society/article/3270940/hong-kongs-west-kowloon-arts-hub-sell-land-parcels-few-years-time-ceo-says.

34 'Transcript of Remarks by the Hong Kong Chief Executive at Media Session before ExCo', 21 May 2024, https://www.info.gov.hk/gia/general/202405/21/P2024052100319.htm.

5: The New Hong Kong

1 Evelyn Cheng, 'China's Xi Says Hong Kong Is Moving "from Chaos to Governance"', *CNBC*, 1 July 2022, https://www.cnbc.com/2022/07/01/china-xi-says-hong-kong-is-moving-from-chaos-to-governance.html.

2 'HKSAR Government Strongly Condemns Slanders, Smears and Divisive Act by anti-China Organisation "Hong Kong Watch" regarding Basic Law Article 23 Legislation', Hong Kong government press release, 21 May 2024.

3 'Hong Kong National Security Police Seize "Pillar of Shame" Statue in Connection with Subversion Case', *SCMP*, 5 May 2023, https://www.scmp.com/news/hong-kong/law-and-crime/article/3219532/hong-kong-national-security-police-seize-pillar-shame-statue-connection-subversion-case.

4 'Hong Kong Home Affairs Chief Says Removal of Artwork Showing

Construction Workers in Yellow Helmets Was Restaurant Owner's Decision',
SCMP, 25 August 2023, https://www.scmp.com/news/hong-kong/society/
article/3232362/hong-kong-home-affairs-chief-says-removal-artwork-
showing-construction-workers-yellow-helmets-was.

5 Senior administrator of a major Hong Kong cultural institution, private
conversation with the author, 28 November 2023.

6 Lisa Movius, '"The Pendulum Keeps Tightening": What Hong Kong's New
Security Law Could Mean for the Art World', *The Art Newspaper*, 20 March
2024, https://www.theartnewspaper.com/2024/03/20/the-pendulum-keeps-
tightening-artists-and-curators-warn-of-dangers-brought-by-hong-kongs-
new-security-law.

7 Ophelia Lai, 'Hong Kong Art Space Raided Twice by Authorities', *Art Asia
Pacific*, 15 June 2021, https://artasiapacific.com/news/hong-kong-art-space-
raided-twice-by-authorities.

8 Private conversation with the author, 3 November 2023.

9 Chris Yeung, 'Censorship Law "Would Not Last"', *SCMP*, 12 November 1994,
https://www.scmp.com/article/95672/censorship-law-would-not-last.

10 'Government Proposes Amendments to Film Censorship Ordinance to
Enhance Regulatory Framework', 24 August 2021, https://www.info.gov.hk/
gia/general/202108/24/P2021082400516.htm.

11 Enid Tsui, 'Hong Kong Movie Industry Body Baffled by Censors'
Requirement for Film's Screening', *SCMP*, https://www.scmp.com/lifestyle/
arts-culture/article/3249078/hong-kong-museum-has-rename-banned-
chinese-film-order-screen-it.

12 Florence Yuk Ki Lee, *Elephant in Castle*, 2021, https://giloo.ist/episodes/1003.

13 Ambrose Li and Enid Tsui, 'Hong Kong's Arts Funding Examiners Will
Be Required to Safeguard National Security, but Aspirants Should Not Be
Deterred by New Rule: Culture Minister', *SCMP*, 12 August 2023, https://
www.scmp.com/news/hong-kong/politics/article/3230893/hong-kongs-arts-
funding-examiners-will-be-required-safeguard-national-security-aspirants-
should-not.

14 Cannix Yau, 'Funding Cuts, Cancelled Shows Leave Hong Kong Arts
Groups Guessing about "Red Lines" Caused by National Security Law',
SCMP, 8 February 2024, https://www.scmp.com/news/hong-kong/politics/
article/3251139/funding-cuts-cancelled-shows-leave-hong-kong-arts-groups-
guessing-about-red-lines-caused-national.

15 ibid.

Art in Hong Kong

16 'Official Record of Proceedings: Wednesday, 18 August 2021', Legislative Council of Hong Kong, https://www.legco.gov.hk/yr20-21/english/counmtg/hansard/cm20210818-translate-e.pdf.

17 Harvey Kong, 'President of Dissolved Hong Kong Independence Party Gets 5 Years' Jail for Secession Offence Tied to Online Posts', *SCMP*, 11 April 2024, https://www.scmp.com/news/hong-kong/law-and-crime/article/3258654/president-dissolved-hong-kong-independence-party-gets-5-years-jail-secession-offence-tied-online.

18 'Man Jailed for Three Months over "Seditious" T-shirt with a Protest Slogan', *The Standard*, 10 January 2024, https://www.thestandard.com.hk/breaking-news/section/4/212285/Man-jailed-for-three-months-over-%2525E2%252580%252598seditious%2525E2%252580%252599-T-shirt-with-a-protest-slogan.

19 Lilian Cheng, 'Court Bans "Glory to Hong Kong". What Is the Song and Why Is it so Controversial?', *SCMP*, 9 May 2024, https://www.scmp.com/news/hong-kong/politics/article/3262057/court-bans-glory-hong-kong-what-song-and-why-it-so-controversial.

20 Flora Drury, 'Hong Kong Arrests Six for Sedition under New Law', *BBC News*, 28 May 2024, https://www.bbc.com/news/articles/c2qq47qdqwlo.

21 Yau, 'Funding Cuts, Cancelled Shows Leave Hong Kong Arts Groups Guessing'.

22 Alvin Lum, 'American Photographer who Covered Hong Kong Protests Denied Entry into City', *SCMP*, 4 June 2020, https://www.scmp.com/news/hong-kong/politics/article/3044660/american-photographer-who-covered-hong-kong-protests-denied.

23 Zuni partnership, 'Hong Kong Belt-Road City-to-City Cultural Exchange Conference 2018 (Asian Strategy): Cultural Think Tanks', *SCMP*, 28 September 2018, https://www.scmp.com/presented/lifestyle/topics/zuni-hkbr-conference-think-tank/article/2165761/hong-kong-belt-road-city.

24 'East-meets-West Centre for International Cultural Exchange', 2021 Policy Address, October 2021, https://www.policyaddress.gov.hk/2021/eng/pdf/publications/14-5/08_Arts-and-Cultural-Exchange-Hub.pdf.

25 'Bauhinia Culture Group Debuts at Guangzhou Cultural Industry Fair 2021', *Global Times*, 6 December 2021, https://www.globaltimes.cn/page/202112/1240803.shtml.

26 'Hong Kong Federation of China Federation of Literary and Art Circles Inaugurated', *Xinhua*, 19 November 2020, http://www.xinhuanet.com/english/2020-11/19/c_139525475.htm.

27 'Welcome Message', Culture, Sports and Tourism Bureau, https://www.cstb. gov.hk/en/about-us/welcome-message.html.

28 'LCQ17: Values Education on National Identity', written reply by the Secretary for Education, Mr Kevin Yeung, in the Legislative Council, 6 April 2022, https://www.info.gov.hk/gia/general/202204/06/P2022040600236.htm.

29 'About Chinese Culture Festival', *Chinese Culture Festival*, https://www.ccf. gov.hk/en/about/.

30 'Government Announces a Range of Measures to Promote Mega Event Economy', Hong Kong government press release, 26 January 2024, https://www.info.gov.hk/gia/general/202401/26/P2024012600739. htm#:~:text=The%20Government%20will%20adopt%20a,of%202024)%20 is%20at%20Annex.

31 Ezra Cheung, '"Chubby Hearts Hong Kong" Art Installation's HK$7.8 million Government Handout Sparks Calls for more Transparency on how Public Cash is Spent', *SCMP*, 17 February 2024, https://www.scmp.com/news/hong-kong/society/article/3252249/chubby-hearts-hong-kong-art-installations-hk78-million-government-handout-sparks-calls-more.

32 'Plenty of Room for Arts Development: Kevin Yeung', *RTHK*, 30 August 2023, https://news.rthk.hk/rthk/en/component/k2/1715835-20230830.htm.

33 Eric Wear, 'Your Risk in Attending Art Basel Hong Kong 2024', September 2023, https://ericottowear6.wixsite.com/art-basel-hk24.

34 Aaina Bhargava, 'Art Basel: Hong Kong Galleries Back Organiser Amid Calls to Cancel Fair over Protests, Coronavirus Emergency', *SCMP*, 1 February 2020, https://www.scmp.com/lifestyle/arts-culture/article/3048469/art-basel-hong-kong-galleries-back-organiser-amid-calls.

35 Eileen Kinsella, 'Pace Has Closed its Beijing Branch Amid Escalating US-China Tensions. Will Other Western Art Galleries Follow Suit?', *Artnet*, 9 July 2019, https://news.artnet.com/market/pace-closes-beijing-gallery-1595935.

36 Marc Glimcher, this and subsequent quotes, interview with the author, March 2024.

37 SCMP Reporters, 'Gustav Klimt Painting Auctioned for US$32 million Was the Subject of a Claim of Ownership just before its Sale', *SCMP*, 26 April 2024, https://www.scmp.com/lifestyle/arts-culture/article/3260536/gustav-klimt-painting-auctioned-us32-million-was-subject-claim-ownership-just-its-sale.

38 Lindsay Dewar and Margaret Hong, 'Auction Analysis: Hong Kong Modern & Contemporary Evening Sales – Spring 2024', *ArtTactic*, https://arttactic. com/product/auction-analysis-hk-spring-2024/.

39 Alicia García Herrero, 'China's Luxury Consumption Story to Stall against Structural Economic Deceleration', *The Corner*, 14 May 2024, https://thecorner.eu/news-the-world/world-economy/chinas-luxury-consumption-story-to-stall-against-structural-economic-deceleration/114586/.

40 Melanie Gerlis, 'Stolen Titian Found at Bus Stop Sells for £15mn', *Financial Times*, 4 July 2024, https://www.ft.com/content/8266cde1-0a52-4d25-8463-1e13a076a09b.

41 Jonathan Crockett, interview with the author, March 2024.

42 Damian Chandler, private conversation with the author, 23 July 2024.

43 Henry Tang, this and subsequent quotes, interview with the author, November 2023.

44 'Anti-LGBTQ Lawmakers Call for Ban on Hong Kong Gay Games, Saying it Poses Threat to National Security', *SCMP*, 1 November 2023, https://www.scmp.com/news/hong-kong/society/article/3240010/anti-lgbtq-lawmakers-call-ban-hong-kong-gay-games-saying-it-poses-threat-national-security.

45 Author's conversation with an art administrator, November 2023.

46 Enid Tsui, 'What Do Chinese Artists Think of Art Censorship in Mainland China? Hong Kong Exhibition Offers an Explicit Examination', *SCMP*, 29 March 2023, https://www.scmp.com/lifestyle/arts-culture/article/3215075/what-do-chinese-artists-think-art-censorship-mainland-china-hong-kong-exhibition-offers-explicit.

47 Billy Tang, interview with the author, December 2023.

48 'The Baer Faxt Talk at the House', panel discussion in Hong Kong on 9 September 2024.

49 Cheung Hok-hang, 'Hong Kong Artists' Shenzhen Exhibitions Look at Cities' Shared Anxieties to Show how Art Connects People Regardless of Geographical Boundaries', *SCMP*, 19 December 2023, https://www.scmp.com/lifestyle/arts-culture/article/3245448/hong-kong-artists-shenzhen-exhibitions-look-cities-shared-anxieties-show-how-art-connects-people.

50 Tozer Pak, interview with the author, December 2023.

51 Ambrose Li, 'Hong Kong Wants to Make a Big Splash in "Art Tech". But what is it? From AI to NFTs, Broad Brush Approach may Need Better Framing, Experts Say', *SCMP*, 19 April 2024, https://www.scmp.com/news/hong-kong/education/article/3259550/hong-kong-wants-make-big-splash-art-tech-what-it-ai-nfts-broad-brush-approach-may-need-better.

52 Wency Chen, 'Tech War: OpenAI to further Block Access by Mainland China, Hong Kong-based Developers', *SCMP*, 25 June 2024, https://www.

scmp.com/tech/policy/article/3267971/tech-war-openai-further-block-access-
mainland-china-hong-kong-based-developers.

53 Eunice Tsang, interview with the author, March 2024.

54 'Researching, Curating and Practising Art in Hong Kong Now', seminar at
the University of Hong Kong, 27 June 2024.

55 Arthur de Villepin, interview with the author, 8 December 2023.

56 Suhanya Raffel, interview with the author, October 2023.

Further Reading

Cheng, Vennes. 'The Misrepresentation of Hong Kongness: The Revamped Hong Kong Museum of Art', *Museum Worlds*, vol.8, no.1 (2020)

Cheng, Vennes. 'The Fleeting Border of Hongkongness in Hong Kong's Contemporary Art', *Hong Kong Studies*, vol.3, no.2 (Spring 2023)

Clarke, David. *China – Art – Modernity: A Critical Introduction to Chinese Visual Expression from the Beginning of the Twentieth Century to the Present Day* (Hong Kong University Press, Hong Kong, 2019)

Dapiran, Antony. *City on Fire: The Fight for Hong Kong* (Scribe Publications, London, 2020)

Ibrahim, Zuraidah and Lam, Jeffie (eds), *Rebel City: Hong Kong's Year of Water and Fire* (World Scientific Publishing Co., South China Morning Post, Singapore, Hong Kong, 2020)

Koon, Yeewan. 'Where Are We Now? M+ and the Uncertain Future of Hong Kong', *October*, no.180 (Spring 2022)

Lau, Jasper. 'Hong Kong Art in the Postcolonial Cultural Context: Book Review of David Clarke's "Hong Kong Art – Culture and Decolonization"' (in Chinese), *Hong Kong Economic Journal* (12 January 2001)

Lim, Louisa. *Indelible City: Dispossession and Defiance in Hong Kong* (Riverhead Books, New York, 2022)

Lo, Sonny Shiu-hing. *The New Politics of Beijing – Hong Kong Relations* (Hong Kong University Press, Hong Kong, 2024)

Vigneron, Frank. *Hong Kong Soft Power: Art Practices in the Special Administrative Region, 2005–2014* (The Chinese University of Hong Kong Press, Hong Kong, 2018)

Wong, Michelle Wun-ting. 'Circulating Abstraction: Exhibiting Hong Kong in Manila, 1961–82', *Ambitious Alignments: New Histories of Southeast Asian Art, 1945–1990* (Power Publications and National Gallery Singapore, Singapore, Sydney, 2018)

Online Resources

Asia Art Archive, aaa.org.hk

Hong Kong Art Archive, arthistory.hku.hk/index.php/resource-centre/hkaa-guide/

M+ Magazine, www.mplus.org.hk/en/magazine/

Microwave International New Media Arts Festival archive, www.microwavefest.net/festival2022/FestivalArchive.html

Further Reading

Index

Note: page numbers followed by n indicate notes.